The Doctor is In/Curable

A mid-forties momma just trying to get through life without sticking her leg to the shower wall.

By D.R. Wright

Contents

Foreword

Fair Warning

DO NOT read this book while

1) Drinking super hot liquids (or any liquids you would not want touching your nasal passages or nasopharynx, or potentially eroding into your brain stem).

2) On the toilet unless that is the only place your children or house people will leave you in peace (actually this is likely a safe venue).

3) In the clinic or other crowded place where you have to hide your laughter.

   Yes, it's that funny.

Dr. Sailaja Nallapaneni, General and Laparoscopic Surgery FRCSC

The Glamorous Life, Family Medicine Style

You know it's the last day of a loooong run of work when you decide to fancy it up a bit to make your face look less dead.

So you put on eyeliner.

Except it's not eyeliner because you broke that weeks ago. So you grab your eyebrow stick-y thing, thinking that will do.

And you put it on in the darkness because the lights are quite frankly too harsh for your tired bleeding eyes to handle quite yet.

You drive to work and get there just as it's becoming light.

Do a quick search in the rearview mirror for the one white pube that grows on your chin between when you've plucked it in the morning and when you get to work. Realizing your post forty metabolism only works well in that one hair follicle.

Then you spot it.

1

Hairy eyelids.

And you realize you didn't get the memo that your eyebrow stick-y thing has filaments in it.

So now you have pube eyelids. Tired. Droopy pube eyelids.

And you feel ready to take on that work day.

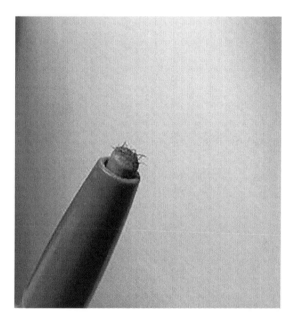

Family Medicine:
A condensed synopsis of my life's profession.

When you finish medical school, and go on to train in a specialty (called "Residency" in Canada and many other places around the world), you look for a good fit for the type of medicine you would like to practice.

For me, Family Medicine was a no brainer. I had been a paramedic in my past life, and although I loved the thrill of being able to help humans in their most emergent times, my soul longed to have a better connection beyond meeting someone in a crisis, getting them to hospital and never seeing them again.

Family doctors are the physicians you see in the community who, in the most basic terms, follow the same population of patients over the long term, weaving through delicate and complex relationships over many many years. The term "Cradle to Grave Medicine" can capture this concept. We work at preventing diseases and managing illnesses as they happen. Organizing further care with our specialist colleagues if what we are seeing is out of our scope of practice. But it is so much more than this.

It is a lifetime of practice, getting to know the deepest and most meaningful parts of other human beings. Connecting with a patient's greatest fears, while working to keep them mentally and physically safe. It is trying to prevent horrible diseases before they happen. Holding another human's trust in you, to walk beside them, and help them get better during their illness journey. It is cuddling babies, and making sure they grow well. It is smiling when someone tells you that they have been free of drugs for two weeks, and cheering them on. It is weighing up options for cancer treatment with someone who knows they have little time left. And it is every instance of heaviness and happiness that happens in life between the moments of wellness and illness. It is a job I feel very privileged to do, and it gives me life. But it also drags me into the depths of the darker sides of my own experience at times, and pulls me into places that I feel uncomfortable being. And this is why the humor. The humor gets me through and where appropriate, I hope it provides my patients with a giggle, even in their darkest times.

Someone once described family medicine as "The Jack of All Trades and Master of None". But I think that explanation robs Family Doctors of all of the ingenuity and skills that they had to develop in areas where wait-times to see specialists, or access to further care is hard to come by, or doesn't exist at all. Especially in the last couple of years, when Covid has pushed us all into having to become creative with our skills, knowledge and ways to get patients the treatment they deserve in a time when access to what they need is not available. Becoming the "Master of Most" is more a statement that I think a lot of us could relate to.

Though my kids would say Family Medicine is my only job (a perception I am trying to change by not working as much), my role as "mom" to two incredible souls, is without a doubt my ride-or-die reason to live. My role as a parent has molded me into a more perceptive physician, but it comes at a terrible cost of feeling and knowing every fear a parent has about their child. Moving forward, I hope to continue to work with passion, without taking away from the needs of my family. Knowing that in life, we are all just trying to get by on any given day. And that I am human. That my capacity to hold the suffering and needs of others is also finite, and that I deserve what I want for my patients as well. Hard to keep in mind when the suffering and need is overflowing.

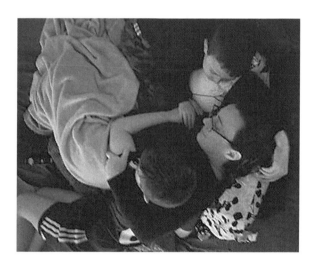

The hilarity of a tired brain (pass the coffee)

Who else is killing this Monday so far? (ie Did not sleep well last night).

Just went to the same Tim Hortons I do daily, and got coffee from the same person I always do. Instead of saying a chirpy and smiley "cheers" (from behind my mask to say thanks), my brain malfunctioned and I announced at the top of my lungs "Change!!!!", as she handed my twenty cents back.

Thankfully I was in my car so no walk of weirdness out of there.

I guess I have to find a new Tim's.

In a new country.

Bum Chafe from your own body fluids: the worst kind of bum chafe.

I got to work today and didn't realize that our "humane" PPE had been restocked.

So I slipped on this "one size fits none", garbage bag thingy that was made for someone with twenty-foot long arms and started instantly shedding 7 pounds of water down my own pants via my own sweat glands (who knew they could work so well?).

The irony is it's waterproof, but I still managed to spill a sip of coffee down my neck before applying my mask.

I see why very premature babies are sometimes put into bags to warm them up, for medical reasons. It's fucking hot (sorry if you don't swear).

And then from the humidity from my own body in a baggie, my shield fogged up, which was awesome given that I was going to do a pap. And about twenty minutes later I felt like I knew what failure to thrive felt like, self-induced, by wearing a bag over my whole body in a poorly air conditioned space.

So cheers to anyone who has to wear a plastic bag thingy with a hole cut in the top of it for your neck, for any period of time. I literally don't know how you do it! I hope you get free Gatorade during your work hour, new underwear hourly and a huge salt lick in your office. I hope someone kindly gives you Penaten samples for the rubbing wet bum chafe. If you are at that time of life with hot flashes, I promise to avenge your death from "sweating" out of a baggy (the weird dehydration equivalent of bleeding out).

In all seriousness if your reality is surviving this for any period of time I am so, so sorry and hope you are ok. You are a total star!

The Big Bang: Near death and no one noticed

So, I almost died today which oddly I can't stop laughing about. Must be the stress come down.

Anyone else feeling grateful to be alive?? How many lottery tickets should I buy?

I was cold in my office and was debating turning up the heat and being warm, versus freezing, but not falling asleep (cause it can get very hot quickly in our offices and it's always a fine balance between "awake brain" and angry cold bum).

So I felt like a genius when I remembered I had my heating pad, (you know you're 43 when you have a heating pad at your beck and call both at home and in the office).

I plugged it in and sat on it (warm bum, cold office = perfect combo). However, as it turns out the heater and the heating pad cord were not the perfect combo. I'm in a new office and I completely didn't notice the location of the wall heater directly below the plug.

11

I heard a loud bang and saw a flash of light. At first I thought I had been shot, which was very confusing as I was still alive and in no pain. I hope you're laughing at this point because I was under my desk when I first smelled the burning and realized it wasn't coming from my body. (As an aside I found a ton of dust and a dead hornet. Nice.)

Needless to say from the photos, the heat through the cord blew a hole in the heater, and completely burnt through one side of the cord.

I have no idea from the pattern on the wall and burst of light how I didn't catch on fire. I am very grateful I didn't die from electrocution via bum for several reasons.

Now to stop for a lottery ticket. Hope to have a glass of wine when I get home. Is there anything else I should be doing on the day I almost died? I have a ton of work to do tonight, but I'm not feeling like that's going to cut it. Did you almost die before? How many lives do we generally get, do you think?

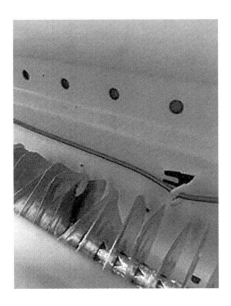

Your "thing"

Trigger warning: if you have a queasy stomach, you might want to skip this (nahhh, don't!)

I remember in residency watching one of my supervisors gag (very subtly I might add), as he lanced an unfortunately large abscess from a rather cheesy armpit.

Picture a water balloon filled with the death of your soul. In cheese form. (Pick a smellier cheese. A good blue cheese). Under immense pressure.

Ok. You've got it.

There was a pungent smell.

Pungent. A good term to use when body parts turn into ooze and then get trapped under a layer of skin, invite bacteria to party, and then fester.

At first a geyser and then a stream of pus and blood oozing from this poor patient's pit. And the patient's pain that went with the procedure made it seem all the more "Nope".

We were also in a hot room, which helped with exactly zero of the aforementioned.

With his professional face forward to the patient, he would explain kindly what he was doing, apply firm but gentle pressure to the now lanced area, and then look away slightly, so that his 'heave face' went unnoticed as the infection drained out. I was standing holding the gauze, soaking up the end of this patient's tension-filled misery. Such a satisfying procedure I thought, because of the instant relief for the patient.

At the end my senior had to "pop out to get something". I knew from his shade of green, that the 'something' was fresh air, head down time, and at least six meters from the cheesy pit.

When it was done, he couldn't "politely and professionally" get out of there faster.

"Well done on not actually vomiting", I felt the need to say. These were my days before kids, before real practice had begun, before my frontal lobe[1] had developed a filter and when it didn't occur to me that mocking a senior resident might not be the coolest, kindest or best thing to help in my professional trajectory

---

[1] Your frontal lobe is responsible for many things. Amongst them should be the ability to rationally weed out things that you can say that might help you vs things that you can say that might harm you.

"It's not the abscess, it's the armpit I can't stand".

"That patient's pit? Or pits in general? Like every pit? Shaved ones? Dry ones? Clean ones?"

"Every axilla is a nightmare for me. A warm damp horror show. I'm not sure why. It just is".

God, of all the things I'd seen as a paramedic I couldn't believe someone could be turned off by an area literally made up of skin folds.

He must have seen me smirking. "Oh you'll find your 'thing'" he said with a smile. "And when you do, I hope you think of this moment and give yourself a small punch in the neck from me".

Fair enough I thought. I've literally seen everything. And nothing was that heave worthy. I would be fine.

But that was a lie.

Because as it turns out, being a paramedic hadn't prepared me for the world of in-hospital medicine. Or family practice land. Where the adrenaline can be less, due to the controlled nature of the situation, the lights bearing down in full and the team of family members and staff watching you in the spotlight, for the more benign presentations.

And there's that constant smell. Of alcohol and "clean" stuff and fear and bad coffee and someone who hasn't brushed their teeth in twelve hours (spoiler: me. What? Our shifts were long and busy!). And somehow that sets the tone for that weird bit of your brain that can't cope with anything, to suddenly be the only part of your brain to show up.

A perfect storm just laying in wait.

And then weird things wobble in. And the parts of your brain that are all muscled up with thoughts of "ohhhh yeah, pus, blood, mucous, body parts falling off? Send it!!! I can take it", shut down completely.

And "Norman", the one area of your brain that can't cope with anything, is suddenly headlining the show. And "Norman" is a serious struggler. Norman is the kid who faints in science class, when the worms held by pins on the black plate thingy come out for dissection. Norman is lovely, but not built for seeing the gross things that most people, to be fair, have no interest in seeing.

I found my "thing" late one night in a small town emergency room. I was doing a shift with one of the family doctors who covered the Emergency Department from time to time.

An ambulance was bringing in someone with "leg trauma".

Trauma was the bread and butter of my past life. I was ready for a half sliced off leg, parts poking and dangling out, something smooshed. A tendon flopping around, a muscle hanging; a bone protruding. But what happened instead was completely different.

A man arrived, on a stretcher, screaming in pain. My preceptor told me to go talk to, and examine the patient while he got the history from the paramedics.

And I was going to. But then I looked at his leg and at the patient who was screaming and almost passing out from pain, and I felt the room closing in.

I started to sweat. I had no idea where my focus was floating. I had these out of body experiences before, so I'm pretty sure I was semi jogging on the spot trying to connect myself to the room and the ground when my preceptor nudged into the side of me and whispered "whatcha doing?" (spoiler: I didn't know what the fuck I was doing apart from trying to re-attach my thoughts to my human body and the room in which I was standing)

He was very kind, quiet and understated and thankfully understanding of a resident currently having a "wonky" episode in front of him.

"Did you get the history?"

"That's a negative," I said (the things Norman says). My brain froze and I was just focussing on keeping myself vertical.

"His knee is wrong-ish" was all I could get out. He took a look at me and said, "maybe you should sit down, out in the hall. I can't fix a knee properly if I have to kick your fainted body out of my working area."

Yeah. Fair enough.

So I sat in the hall in a corner. Head down. Pretending to do an extra important job existing between the chair and the floor whenever someone walked by. And then I gathered myself together, feeling absolutely ridiculous, took a deep breath in and bolted back into the action.

"Sorry" I whispered as I saddled up to my preceptor.

"It's ok", he answered. "Are you ok? Cause I'm going to need your help in a second?"

I felt fine. But then I looked down again. And thought I might jump out of my own soul. The wavy lines in my vision started to re-appear. My brain was actively trying to find an escape route. I was spending every ounce of my awareness trying to kick Norman out and find the part of my brain that can deal with really bad shit. I was having a hard time making that happen.

The patient was now a bit more comfortable having been given something for pain, but still making the face people make when something is horribly wrong with their body. The face was not helping, and I started floating above myself again.

Summoning all of my strength, while my preceptor was doing "all of the everything" needed to prepare to correct this situation while I stood there bobbing in space, I looked down again at the patient's left knee.

His knee cap, through various methods of trauma that I missed, was laying on the side of his leg. I don't mean lying as in "on a towel on a beach on a holiday", I mean forcefully displaced from the lovely and anatomically comfortable spot that resides between the bottom of one's femur and the tops of one's tibia.

His knee cap was nowhere near his knee cap home. It had been bumped out of place and was now bulging out of the side of his mid leg. This knee cap had no fucking business being there.

His angry muscles were absolutely agreeing with me. Writhing and pulling, and threatening to snap at any moment. Their movements likely contributing to the face of misery the patient was still making. Norman took another look at that face, and the curtains started closing in again.

Everything about this knee cap, the muscles spasming around it and the pain the patient was in, made me feel like I could die imminently.

My preceptor was getting ready to inject the patient with medications, the kind that would sedate him without getting him too close to death. Pain medications strong enough to take the horrible edge off, but not to prevent the horror that would happen when popping it back in. The extra bonus was the amnesia the patient would experience. I was actively wondering how I could experience the same amnesia for what I was about to hear and see and feel.

I honestly don't know what his words or directions were. But I was going to somehow help hold the leg so that he could take the kneecap, which was currently making a run for its life, and knock it back into place. Working against spasming, severely angry muscles, this takes a lot of strength. What I remember was a command of "now", doing something that involved movement and pushing and a loud grotesque thump/clump of the knee cap popping back into place.

For a moment I thought the thump was the sound of my brain dying. I realized this wasn't the case when sweat ran down my bum, and I knew that I was still sadly very much alive.

And then I stood there frozen. While commotion scuttled around me at a fairly high speed. I'm sure the Norman part of my brain tried to make me look relaxed and happy to reassure the patient. I'm sure he woke up to me standing there. Still partially holding his leg, sweating like a maniac and staring without blinking with a forced smile on my face. His recount to his family later would be "and then they popped it back in, and I felt immediate relief and then realized the kid who fell through the cracks of medical school and somehow got into the residency program was grinning at me like an idiot while still holding my leg".

I'm assuming my preceptor helped me out. That knee cap area of my brain has died.

Thankfully, examining knees doesn't bother me at all. Only the knees where the cap has decided it no longer needs to live in its home.

And people with dislocated kneecaps never just "wander into" family medicine land. They are an emergency trip 100% of the time.

So a swift punch to the neck for wandering knee caps as it turns out.

And for sputum or bodily fluids that one brings in a tissue or jar to show me[2]. Another small punch for removing toenails. I would tell you that story, but the time it would take to recover in a sanitarium would preclude me from finishing this book.

---

[2] While in medical school one of the Respirologists teaching us was old school. He used to command that everyone with a productive cough have a pot beside them to spit into on the ward. A "sputum pot" sat filled with gunk handily beside each patient. When rounding on patients he would then open the pot of sputumy death and smell it, announcing what infection he thought the patient might have. I'm not sure about how you feel about this, but I felt very badly. This almost scuttled my chances of being successful in medical school, as I would nearly die every time it happened. I mean really, what could be more gag worthy and horrendous when a quick swab would tell us what the patient "actually" had. If you bring me a pot of something wet, I hope it did not come from your respiratory tract or your nasal passages.

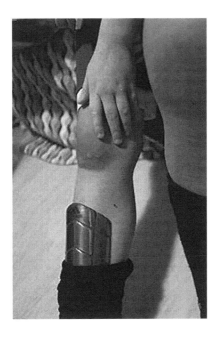

Gratitude to and connection with colleagues

Misery loves company as much as success loves having a crowd to celebrate with.

Not many hold within the scope of their daily work, the pressure that is keeping others well. Though others can relate to our line of work, there are few I know outside of the business who have tried to resuscitate a fellow human being at 3am while a family member goes through the trauma of the worst day of their lives. Or have delivered a baby, welcoming a new life into a tumultuous world. Or have been responsible for keeping someone alive as their heart fails to pump, or their lungs fail to work. All physicians have been through make or break moments in someone else's life journey. And although we branch into doing different jobs, we all know what that stress, and loss and fear looks like. And we all know what the best days, and triumphs afford as well. And I think this draws us together as colleagues and humans. To keep from losing myself in the world of the health of others, my creative side is drawn to writing as a stress outlet. And often that is shared within groups of other physicians. In snippets here, my thoughts are shared with them, often in the time of Covid, reaching out to let them know that I see them, and I feel them, in this collective time of struggle. It gives me comfort, and I hope it provides something in that way for them as well.

 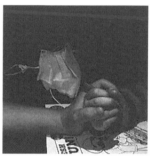

When you hit the wall of working: ode to my colleagues (aka: Aired out vulvas, "Go on then, make my mom proud"!)

Yesterday was so so hard. I think when you get to see the light at the end of the tunnel sometimes your body and mind kind of give up.

Yesterday I genuinely thought, I cannot do one more day of family medicine during Covid. I was so, so burnt out I considered calling in sick for my final day before the holidays (which I haven't done since Covid started...thank you "phone billing" for being able to keep me working even when in bed sick....which I know all of us have done).

But not today!!!

Today I woke up after a terrible sleep and gave zero shites!!! Today I knew, only 8 more hours to go before FIVE whole days of freedom (well you know, family doc freedom, the kind that requires you to check your inbox every day....lol...but still

FIVE days patient-free! and in peace/chaos/rage vs happiness with my little family).

So when I drove through Tim's this morning, with horrendous bags under my eyes and "flame red" conjunctiva I gave them my best smile and a tip when I collected my coffee. Being early, I sauntered over to the garbage/recycling bins, emptying out my cars worth of litter thinking *Woohoo, an extra job done and the day hasn't even begun!* I felt smug and full of life!!! (or at least jittery and full of caffeine!)

When I then drove off with my coffee cup on the roof of the car, I thought "who gives a crap it's my last day!" and smiled my big moronic smile to the confused looks of those at the Tim's window who had just seen me five minutes earlier.

When I got to work and found my pants were covered in cat hair from leaving them on the dresser last night, I thought "not to worry" and gleefully dealt with what would have done me in the day before, with a snicker to myself and scotch tape.

When two challenging patients were booked in a row, I refused to think any soul stealing could happen, leaned into the challenge, and legitimately thought that I was able to help both of them.

When I sat on a piece of chocolate, I looked at it and pondered, *If someone wants to think I shat myself, then be my guest!*

When the pap leg/foot stirrup thingy (I love how they are called a stirrup, like we are going on a fancy pony ride to a vagina theme park)got stuck, I didn't lose my cool, instead, I re-shifted the patient and found her cervix without any discomfort or embarrassment.

When I looked in the mirror and noticed one entire green salad leaf was covering my front tooth I smiled to myself and put my mask back on, "thank you Covid Silver Linings."

And when my steam ran out at the end of the day, and my boys sent me this photo of our train table and the snow magic they had made, I sighed, thankful that my children are healthy, that my husband is a kind and lovely gent (with weird taste in sweaters), and that my kids only bicker every other second.

As I was heading out, I felt grateful for the awesome fish and chips place right beside my work. As I carried a huge pile of food and pop in my arms, and my underwear elastic gave out and then my gitch worked its way down to my knees while I walked (thank goodness I was wearing scrub pants), I didn't panic but remembered the words of my mom (who passed away 3 years ago), "you should always give your vagina an airing" (why is this a thing?????...oh sigh, bless my mom and her weird medical things based on nothing), and put my head up and soldiered on thinking, I hadn't remembered to do that yet today!

And finally as I got home with arms full of work bags, and parcels and a child's backpack I had found in the back seat (which had an odd squish to it), I felt so much gratitude walking through the front automatic doors of our building thinking I was finally heading for a rest with my family.

And when I got stuck and pulled back by the cord of the said backpack in the automatic door, it was like a jolt from the universe to remind me.

Some of you are working these holidays. Some of you are stuck doing this, some of you have offered to take extra shifts, to give those celebrating a holiday that you don't, some peace with their family in the most selfless way.

My family thanks you with all of our heart.

Thank you for pushing through during such an incredibly trying time. For risking your health for ours and for missing your family so that ours can have peace, reassurance and help.

Thank you. We are all here with you if you need us.

Love, a grateful family doc (and her glass of vino!)

Stay safe (and don't forget the daily vagina airing as per my mother)

D.R. Wright

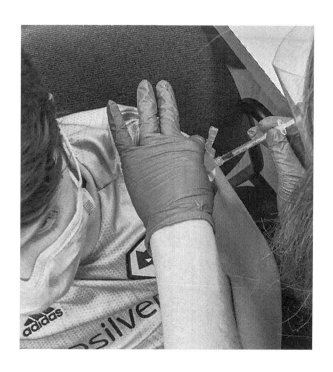

A Break from burnout: When it takes forever to find kindness for yourself.

To all those struggling.

I. See. You.

"For medical reasons this patient will be unable to attend work. This will be reassessed in two weeks"

Sometimes it was two, or three, sometimes four weeks. Often the notes got re-written. A new date set. Extensions in time. Healing slowing down the 24 hours of a clock, to intervals that weren't sufficient to heal a broken mind.

Covid anxiety breaking those who had been holding themselves together with tape but now found with people panic buying, that they could no longer find any. All toilet paper, and pieces that could stick oneself together being pilfered. Snatched up. Nothing left to hold one as one anymore.

Before Covid, I would write this statement often enough. Time off would come easily "written". Prescribed. Support given.

Divorces, someone struggling through an illness, an unwell child, someone saddled with anxiety, stress. A complete mental mis-hap. Neurons letting them down. Chemicals misfiring under duress.

Covid hit and I began writing it all the time.

From daily, to multiple times daily.

Appointments overflowed. I created a "stamp" in our electronic records. Efficiency toward those needing a break from production.

Calls coming in relentlessly. "Hello, family medicine land. I need to be booked in for urgent time off".

Piles of letters.

20 patients a day, mixed into 30. Overflowing, piled on top of one another in the schedule. A gross need to keep up. A heavy need not to fail my patients.

A mental health system in a province where there is no oncall specialist for mental health. Where the Crisis Team is also in crisis.

Sore throat and headaches booked. Anxiety and depression; the real reasons after 15 mins of dealing with the other reason.

So far behind.

Notes left unfinished. Piled on top of notes left unfinished.

Hearing myself over and over " It's ok. Three weeks in a lifetime is no time at all if it brings you peace. If it starts the healing. If it enables you to get help. Take the time. Invest in yourself. Find some balance. I support you".

Then. Hitting the wall.

Standing in an office not knowing where to look next.

Staring at my hands. Alcohol on, washing away any ability to concentrate through the endless relentlessness of need.

Doing jumping jacks to connect myself with the room.

Looking from inbox to schedule.

Piles of despair.

Pile ups of waiting people. Dying while waiting for Covid to end. Their cancers told to wait. "Stop growing a bit while we get this Covid thing under control".

"Hello family medicine land. Have you heard from my specialist yet, my cancer has not taken the advice to stop growing. I think it needs to come out".

Breaking while smiling.

Breaking while reassuring.

Just one more phone call to remind them their results haven't been left behind. We have just not yet heard about when someone can see them.

"Hello family medicine land can you send my mom home in one piece tonight. She can't read more about Covid, and our talking is hurting her brain. Her patients are making her worried. The system is stretching her so much that we can no longer find her. She needs total silence at night. We need our mom's voice".

A note written to myself. In the one empty recess of my mind. Along with "you are replaceable to everyone but your children": "For medical reasons this patient will not be returning to work. This will be reassessed in eight weeks".

A locum booked.

Time taken scarily without pay.

Time to find myself. Find some creative space.

Speak to my partner and my children.

A lot. With kindness and full presence.

A present.

A gift.

To myself.

"I support you. Sorry it took me so long to do that".

Update: D.R. Wright Is All Right

Off for five days already and the stress has come down. My brain is finally slowing down and relaxing itself. A plan for a different looking schedule for when I return is in place.

I am happily reading. I've taken my prescription of Nutella (and Cipralex). It's raining outside. My kids are piddling around.

All is well (I mean it. If you make it to the end of this, you also get time off).

Lifting your heavy hearts with an underwear mystery

There's so much heaviness lately. I'm not trying to take away from the heaviness. I realize though sometimes it comes from a place of ignorance and desperation.

So trying to pick our spirits up a little. Knowing we are all human. I've missed diagnoses I'm sure. I say that in sadness, regret and fear. It's never been out of laziness or hesitation to see a patient. Do you know what your family doc has access to imaging/testing-wise during a pandemic? (hint, it was very little before the pandemic…or at least where I am)

And you have too.

Missed a diagnosis.

Had a distraction.

Lost your soul over it.

Sadly.

That's the ONE thing we all have in common. And if you think it's not, it's either because you started your first shift ten minutes ago, or someone else has stepped in to preserve your humanity and done a really good job.

But you are human. And sad shit happens. Sometimes way more than anything you prepare for.

You see someone one afternoon. Then they die that night. No symptoms.

So I'm trying to lighten the load (but doing a shite job), by telling you that today at work, I had to ditch my underwear.

Thank goodness it was after my only in-person visit (on my paperwork day...when I'm not supposed to see anyone.....and be working from home)...but I arrange it that way to see more patients in-person safely and suck up the lost paperwork time.

I'm not telling you why I had to ditch my underwear midway through the clinic today.

Until someone admits they've had to as well.

Hope every single one of you is feeling well supported, and getting breaks (and checking your underwear).

Working on Wellness with cake mixes: What to do when you get a weird death threat type of letter in your inbox about Covid?

Wellness tips on how to cope with death threats, for those completely haggard and burnt out (based on zero actual wellness evidence, but based on my day yesterday and what worked for me).

1. Go to the gym. Rage it out!!! Or fast walk, (complaining the whole time your legs hurt and have stress toots that you still have to get

out despite the other person in the gym)…..
your decision.

2.   Notice that a patient is just outside the gym window. Drop to the ground. Lay flat. Roll. To where you can peek up until they are gone. Roll back to the gym.

Act naturally. Move In harmony with the world so no one notices.

Come home and have a glass of wine, coffee, tea, or water, that hits HARD.

Dance to "Murder She Wrote" and hit your best late 20's club dance moves. By yourself. Be ashamed about how much sweat that dance has created (but secretly pleased, because the bum sweat was refreshing).

Roll into bed tired. Eat two rice cakes. Realize this is not nearly enough.

Cupboard it up.

Find a boxed cake.

Make it despite missing 2/3 eggs*.

Eat. That. Mo. Fo. Raw.

Risk bad food-related diseases but relish the fact that it tastes like HEAVEN but also like baking soda.

Maybe your reflux won't be that bad.

Fall asleep knowing you did what you could.

And that you could try harder tomorrow.

But that you wouldn't because "doing what you could" is award worthy in these Covid times

Crawl into bed. Realizing the raw cake was a bad idea.

Feel well for the decisions you have made tonight.

They will either (food) poison you or make you stronger.

Follow me for more post death-threat advice.

*this is not medical advice- if you haven't figured out not to do what I say by now, then you might be in need of help.

This doesn't look like the model in the photo: Buying Bathing suits off of the internet during Covid

1 out of 10 bought will be flattering

2 will not fit your boobs properly...thank you breastfeeding for two different cup sizes.

2 will not fit your bottom properly...or they might, if you like half your bum hanging out in an unflattering "squeezed out of the toothpaste tube" kind of way.

1 will say it's your size but will actually be made for a child.

1 will come clearly made of flammable material. And if it fits nicely, then you will likely take your chances during bbq season.

1 will look like that sticky crotchy thing has been used before.

1 will give you a rash after trying it on. Again if it looks good, you will overcome it with some antihistamines.

1 will be see-through. But only where your pannus is.

Most will look completely different than the model in the photo.

1 will make you wonder how you actually are supposed to get it on without compromising your ability to breathe.

1 you will need to be cut free from after taking one too many wrong turns with the strappy bits.

All this to say I just bought two new bathing suits.

Hope one is "the one". And congrats, someone else will get a free suit from my pile o' rejects some day.

(awesome suit....and yes, doctors wear Bikinis!!!!! It took me two times of wearing to realize I was tying the top upside down...sigh)

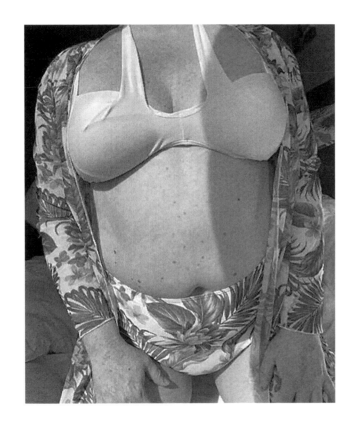

Surprise! Time to get moving!

Do you ever feel like your life is really a scripted comedy?

Like the Truman Show. But the no budget, made in a Canadian basement version?

Ok, don't judge but I'm two weeks into being off and I've gone totally crazy!!!!!! Well not completely. I have been at the same outdoor spa twice in two weeks (and have made really good friends with a huge bottle of Nutella).

To be fair, the first time I booked the spa it was a gift to my hubby.

But he "shy'd out" and sent me instead.

The second time I had booked for myself to write.

It's only $57 all in for a FULL day of access to a "no talking" zone which is all outdoors on a lake! It's got saunas and hot and cold pools and hammocks as far as the eye can see.

But they are so fully booked that they only release these single day passes one at a time. Thus the two different days in two different weeks.

My goal was to go and write a lot.

For a full day.

Out of the apartment. Away from the kids asking for goldfish every 5 seconds and my guilt of not doing something with them. Every. Single. Second. Of a beautiful sunny day.

My awesome hubby was all in! (again).

So I went. And wrote a ton while sitting by the water watching two ducks just doing fucking nothing with their lives but mill about in the water for two whole hours. IN TOTAL SILENCE (yup I'm shouting "total silence" because it was amazing!!!!).

And so I decided to take an hour break from writing. Grab some water, and move about and ended up finding these amazing wooden lounge chairs in the woods (they have mosquito killers so no bugs!).

They were padded with yoga mats and so so comfy. So I lay down, in my bathrobe (yup I robed it up!) pulled it up over my head and drifted off to the sound of the wind and the warmth of the sun on my body.

Then I heard a woman's voice.

And it kept on talking.

Despite the no talking policy.

So I sat up and looked at where it was coming from.

A platform like mine. But in the middle of what I now recognized to be a circle of platforms in the woods.

I thought they were just other lounging spots in this awesome outdoor space.

But as it turns out:

It's a yoga class and I'm frigging sleeping in the middle of it.

So I spring up completely unprepared in every way possible.

Trying to fit in totally nonchalantly. Drool firmly wiped from my face.

I shrug off my gigantic mom robe and proceed to do yoga in the most inappropriate bathing suit of all time. One of the ones you buy online and it's one size fits none, but you've paid your $20 and there's no turning back.

Under a thick robe or laying solo on a hammock my bathing suit was incognito. But robe off, and now doing fucking downward dog with 'Deborah' coming in hot right behind me and 'Patricia' directly in front of me, my steal of an online purchase was:

Letting.

Me.

Down.

Let's say it's nice for the pool side if you're feeling adventurous. Quite low cut, holding breastfeeding boob a) which is a different size then breastfeeding boob b) barely back with its thin top over the neck bit-y thingy piece. In a thin layer of, what online looks like material, but in-person looks like rice paper.

And she's saying things like "bend the knee and then lift directly up into the air".

None of my body goes directly up into the air.

None of it.

Like the last time I tried, I heard my hip audibly say "no".

And I do love yoga, but it's been a while.

A long long while.

And for everyone else it's clearly only been since this morning.

So we are leaning over, and bending backward. And my bathing suit is actually entering orifices unintentionally while I stretch. And I know Debbie can see my shaving rash, cause I can see the inside of Patricia's soul in front of me.

And the sun is shining behind us, and I'm so self-conscious of the material being see-through along my bum line, that I'm already practicing a formal apology to anyone who might have had to glimpse it.

And I really have to pee, and there's this fold yourself in half move, and there's pubes everywhere

(because again I thought "solo in a bathrobe all day", and who has the time for shaving?), and my bladder is willing itself not to do an "oops" in the middle of child pose.

So it lasts forever. And I'm feeling super boss for making it through. Swimsuit, minus one boob protector lost in the process (and on the forest floor for all to see), intact!

Go to the Nordic spa. Live your best life. Have no one talk to you. Read a book. Drink the wine.

Do not sit in the yoga circle though unless you fucking mean it.

Home Warm Wax: A scathing review (but not for the reasons you would think).

I'm sharing this as a service to humanity. No matter how desperate you get, just don't.

For those as bored and hairy as I am.

Disclaimer, I'm not normally this weird but apparently it becomes acceptable during social restrictive measures, with nothing else to do on a Friday night, to write about the horrendous things we do to ourselves.

I'm not a virgin to waxing so it wasn't a frightening prospect. The wax itself smelled good enough; kind of like pine sap mixed with hope. I made Jon smell it and he drifted into a pleasant haze, thinking dreamily about the days when we would camp without children (and by camp, I mean sit in a trailer in Wales and drink with friends).

I warmed it up as instructed and, apart from scalding my skin on the first go, which wasn't ideal, I was smugly thinking I was a pro already.

And that's because I hadn't started yet.

The pain was searing, but tolerable. My comparison is always to either gallstones or a human head exiting my body. I'm not going to say I have a high pain threshold, because I'm not sure what that means (and likely I don't), but it wasn't too bad. It was almost satisfying removing layers of quarantine growth. Almost cathartic. But that was only the first strip.

What they don't tell you on the box, is that likely you are actually using real tree sap, and if you haven't taken two years of leg waxing theory and application technique, then you are going to make an absolute fucking mess.

No biggie I thought, I'll just do it and then clean it up. Except halfway through, the wax hardened and I had to heat it again. No biggie, I'll just tiptoe to the microwave, maneuvering on the outsides of my feet, only as there was a little wax stuck to the bottom of my foot. And by little, I mean a huge frigging glob that is now on every second foot of the apartment floor.

And it won't come off.

Which would be fine, if I didn't ever want to travel through the apartment again, or if we didn't have two very hairy cats currently shedding.

My left leg then hurt a lot more than my right. Perhaps I had lost the ability to cope by that point, or perhaps it's because two of my fingers literally glued together while doing my left leg and I panicked wondering what I would tell my colleagues in emergency when I showed up with my lobster claw of a hand.

Also it didn't really work. For every 10 leg hairs it pulled out, it left two. So now my legs look like my father's head and I'm going to have to shave them anyway. No biggie.

Except it was a biggie because my legs stuck together in the shower, which was unpleasant to resolve. The razor also wouldn't work through the clumps of wax stuck to my legs.

So now I'm laying in bed, my legs are stuck to the sheets despite showering, and I have wax all over the bathroom which is making my anxious feelings about cleanliness boil over.

So in summary you need to either shave or stay hairy. Two clear choices.

Now in all seriousness how do I get the wax off my counter? Tips wanted. As soon as possible.

D.R. Wright

"Raise hands, pull up hard": When the stress bloats mean you need help taking your scrubs off at night.

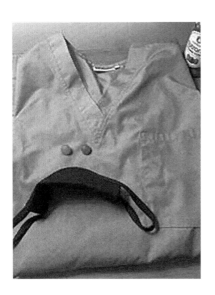

A few days ago, I realized a disheartening decision had to be made. I needed to order new scrubs. It was finally time to come to terms with the fact that the old ones were no longer fit for their purpose.

Bought in a fury off of Amazon, during a scary time when we all knew that wearing scrubs could afford the easiest and safest barrier between work-life germs and homelife children, taking them off at the front door and stuffing them into the wash right away. Happily coming apart at the seams as they went through the rinse cycle(I decided to go the "cheap route" with the company I purchased them from), my slightly thinning scrubs had become part of my daily routine. The tiniest bit of comfort and control for me in a time of madness. Like a new friend. Except my new friend was starting to cause frank ischemia of my gut every time I wore them.

As it turns out, the motivation to get fit for a beach holiday in February 2020, right before the onslaught of the virus hit the world, would not last into March, when the fear of a pandemic would make me eat all of my feelings (on the regular).

I realized that a) it was no longer reasonable for Jon to have to help me take my shirt off at the end of the day after my arms would inevitably get stuck somewhere between the 12 o'clock over my head position, provoking my reflexive shout to help get my stuck head out of the head hole AND b) it was no longer acceptable to live on the edge at work wondering when I was going to bust through my crotch while bending over to grab something.

All of the elastic waist bands (thumbs up for those) that came with my size small scrubs had given out a couple of months ago, and it was only a matter of time before something else might give. I had flashbacks to a time in university when I was wearing these super cool but super tight plaid pants, and I did a "fame" leap outside of a lecture hall (fuck knows why), and my trousers just literally burst off of me.

I'm not up to fame leaping anymore, besides that's not the kind of thing for a senior patient venturing out of the house for the first time during a pandemic to see by accident.

So I ordered again online. Not so much because I enjoy the feeling of fabric mixed with flame retardant and lost hope, and not because I am not worried about how such cheap clothes might have been made. But because, now that there are more than 1.5 cases of Covid in our province, I am a little bit more shy about going anywhere public to try on clothing that might be of a better, more ethically made quality. Also, I know that the delivery man must live in my building.....delivering what I want before I've even ordered it.

So I went into my past orders from the online shop and hit "Re-order" literally only changing my past selection by one size. Ten minutes later when they arrived, I popped them on the dresser, excited that my insanely early start the next day would at least be in extreme, made from paper, guilt, and elastic waistband comfort.

What happened this morning is I got up at 5:45 AM, changed in the dark so as to not wake anyone up, and slipped on my new wardrobe that I had pitched into the dryer the night before to make it less crunchy and stiff.

I thought I was still a bit delirious when I put it on this morning, in basically what I consider the middle of the night, and plodded on despite my pants traveling down to my ankles every two steps. As it turns out, with the brand I ordered, one extra size is actually 7 extra sizes. The shirt sits on my dresser. I tried it on. It feels like tent canvas and is tent shaped...so I'm going to have to wait to grow into that. Saying it's a moo moo is understating both the size and design ever so slightly.

Good thing about the pants, they no longer cause my bowel to hemorrhage. Bad thing about the pants, they have a drawstring and I have to tie it around twice, roll the top over, and still the legs are three people wide. So basically I'm a comfortable clown at work, with pants seven sizes bigger than the shirt I still cannot get off on my own at the end of the day.

Please be kind to your family doctors, they are suffering in ways you will never understand, just trying to get dressed for work.

(And if you're having abdominal pain during the time of covid, before you book in to see us, please make sure it's not just because your pants are too tight.....'cause gas pains are for real my friends...and so is a bowel infarction from denying that your waistband no longer fits your current frame).

Wanting to be a mommy (having sweet little lads)

After a late night working at home it is now 6am when my three year-old boy says: "when I grow up can I be a mommy? Can I be you"?

My bitter heart melts as I try to make out his sweet sweet face through my sleep encrusted eyes ☺

Does anyone else feel like they have to work like an absolute banshee to take a week off of work only to return to a massive pile of work (one that seems impossible to accumulate in the time gone)? #familydoclife

(I did tell him that he shouldn't give up his goal of becoming the very hungry caterpillar).

 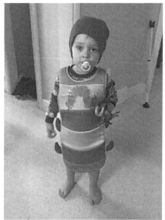

Texts from home.

Anyone else have something from the: "When mom's not home" series?

This one is entitled, 'Dead fly on the couch' (at least it's a clean bra).

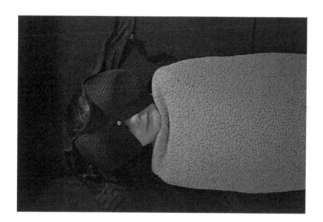

"Hairy Vagina" shouts

I still recoil from my then three year-old yelling "mom your vagina is sooo hairy" in the bathroom stall of a Chapters bathroom. I'm sure the person beside me was happy to know the state of my being.

Another time when someone passed gas beside us in a bathroom stall (likely again at Chapters), the same son shouted "someone just tooted really really loud and didn't say excuse me!" A faint voice beside us in the stall "excuse me". A faint voice back as my soul died "sorry". My son said "why did you say sorry mom? That was rude".

Those moments in time when you are thinking "lawd throw me a bone"! And then figuring out how to buy time in a stall so that you don't have to see this person face to face ever in the existence of your life. Knowing they are likely watching the door when you come out of the washroom from the coffee section judging your whole existence."

D.R. Wright

She's got diamonds on the soles of her ballsack

Today was a shit show in family medicine land. Hope it makes you smile.

As the storm ended, my youngest put his seven-year old arm around my shoulder and said "mom, you're as rich to me as a diamond-crusted ballsack"

No one will know precisely what that means. I hate the term ball sack (so they use it all the time), and I would think a diamond-crusted one would be ouchy.

But in the moment it was said with such love, as we looked at this view. And I thought, I'll take it. When you live with all boys, sometimes a diamond-crusted scrotum is all you can hope to be.

D.R. Wright

Contraception that the whole family can play?

As a physician I wonder if sometimes we might be a little too open in our family.

My eight year-old: why do you have to go to the doctor today?

Me: no big reason, mommy just has to have something done.

My eight year-old: why?

Me: umm...well...just because...it's no big deal

My eight year-old: But why do you have to go to the hospital?

Me: 'cause that's where the doctor is

My eight year-old: but I feel worried, what's happening?

Me: nothing big, mommy is just having something placed inside so that she doesn't have any babies anymore

My eight year-old: what are you having placed inside?

Me: nothing big. Just a small little device

My eight year-old: an iPad?

Me: no honey not an iPad

My eight year-old: oh, that's too bad.

Road trip: Minus the road

My husband planned a "massive RV road trip" for the first three days of my vacation, to take our boys away so that I could rest alone.

What's hilarious about it is that it's 20 minutes away. He knows I'm all about the campfire (we live in an apartment), so he planned it there so that I could join them if I felt up to driving 20 minutes away, in the evenings for a fire.

What's even more awesome than his kind gesture (after watching his wife quite frankly slowly meltdown in family medicine land under the weight of the volume of work), is that I think he's totally uncomfortable driving such a big beast. He never ever camped as a kid in huge campervans.

So their epic RV trip will be from the lot of the RV place 200 feet across the road to the KOA campground. Twenty mins from our home.

I'm feeling like my family is very Chevy Chase "American Vacation"-style. The kids pile in excitedly, amongst the twenty boxes of stuff they've packed for three days, hubby fires up the engine, everyone cheers, they drive 5 feet and "kids weeeeeeeeeeeeee've arrived!!!!". Toot toot.

Motherhood: Frustration and Gratitude.

For anyone struggling with the mom tiredness and the looking after parents exhaustion and work and more work. I see you.

The minutes can move so slowly. Sweet when kisses are given and small hands are playing with your hair. But stress, child sickness, homeschooling due to Covid etc etc all make the time tick tock much slower.

Sleepless nights and the hands of time never move, or so it seems.

But somehow amongst the infinite joy and yet torture of being constantly responsible for someone else's wellness, and goodness and happiness and direction, time creeps in. And fools you.

And you are no longer looking at fumbly toes the size of baby carrots. Or getting kisses where drool and slop makes up 90% of them. But instead pecks on the cheek and fast goodbyes.

Time does pass. And it does fly.

Hold it when you can, even in frustration or tiredness, and be so grateful for the things that you live for.

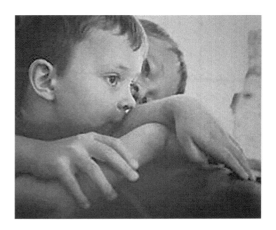

Make this make sense!

My eight year-old lad popped home from school today and proudly announced "I found out today I'm a virgin"! (what are eight year-olds talking about at school these days?)

Fucking fish tanks.

How do I get two shrimp out of a fish tank without my kids noticing?*

....wait for the egg nightmare at the end of the video (sorry, no video for you, as this is a book, but I will find a horror shot of one of the shrimp instead to show you).

The dreaded fish tank.

I don't mind fish. But since having children, I wonder how my parents not only survived but prospered at keeping our fish tank and fish around for so long.

Three times, we have owned a fish tank with children. Two of those times our children have pleaded to have a pet, and after refusing a horse, dog or dinosaur, this is what we have given in to.

Seems like a great idea the first few days when there is extra life in the house and the water is bright and clear and everyone is excited to see how the fish are doing every two minutes.

Seems like a less great idea a week later, when the "ill- looking fish" from the first day starts floating upside down, and then gets stuck to the filter.

Struggling as the other fish peck at him, you tell yourself as you notice, but are running out the door (wanting to distract your kids from the circle of life before you), that you will deal with it before the kids get home.

But then you forget.

And then one of them notices. And it's hard to explain why fish upside down means the fish goes in the toilet.

The first time this happened, our oldest shocked us by being completely and unforgettably heartbroken. He was five, and it totally rocked his world. He said things like "he never got to know us!!!" And "he never got to say goodbye to his family!" and cried for four hours before crying himself to sleep. We were genuinely shocked at how hard he took it.

We said never again.

Then with every move we sold the fish tank in a garage sale (good luck suckers), and then a year or so later, when everyone around us was getting a puppy, we caved to the pet pressure and got another one.

Which is how we are here again.

Except this time, the fish buying wasn't supervised by me. And things have gotten a bit out of control.

We have a shrimp. Which I am genuinely afraid of.

They are like spiders of the sea.

And if you wait until the side view you will see that she is full of mini shrimp eggs.

So when Noah said "mom the fish lady gave us a pregnant one" and looked thrilled, I had to put on my best happy person impersonation, while realizing that my death by shrimp was always inevitable and I should just lean into what the universe has planned for me.

And I'm sure they will all scramble like spiders do when their 7 million eggs hatch.

And one will find its way to my bed.

And I will die. Like I almost did in a shower in Malaysia (my fave place), when a flying cockroach landed on my eyelid, without my glasses on and then put his crawly things on my eye. And all I could do was smack the air, and my face, and yell, in complete myopic blindness.

I guess at least I won't have to worry about the next phase of the fish tank.

Which is in about four weeks when zero shits are given about it, life gets busy, things start to grow on the walls, and the "made to last ten minutes filter" that the store no longer makes for your tank size, shorts and dies.

If you like fish and fish tanks, then sorry for my rant. And please let me know. In about 2 months we will have a tank for sale.

Edit. My oldest informed me the shrimp has shed its "skin" and is now even bigger. Said skin is stuck to the filter with one of his? legs? So basically he's growing fuckking super powers. Someone will need to avenge my death.

P.S. I know the black and white photo is of a crab. The blurry photo is of the shrimp. He/she has been missing for months. He/she is likely in my ear canal and I have not figured out how to take a clear shot of that.

A toxic spill at work. Shit in the Bin.

Parenting: lowering your expectations for humanity? Have your expectations increased or relaxed since becoming a parent?

Warning: This story contains references to human stool in places where it really, quite frankly, has no business being. If you find poo conversations crass, or the worst form of humor, then you might want to skip this one.

Yesterday, while working in family medicine land, one of our clinic staff, calmly but disgustedly announced "there is a poo in one of the garbage cans in one of the exam rooms".

I pictured a small nugget from a diaper that had been dumped, rolling its way into the bottom of the bin. This sometimes happens as we all know, when you haven't wrapped that diaper package (you make post baby poonami), tightly enough.

No biggie I thought.

This was incorrect.

It was a full sized adult shit. Wrapped in the exam table paper, as if someone had tried to daintily package what was definitely not supposed to be left in our bin. The smell and head protruding through our cheap paper gave it away though. It was like someone had a kind thought, with a shitty delivery.

I have full compassion for someone who finds themselves in the position where they cannot make it from the exam room table to the bathroom directly across the hall. I myself have been in similarly tricky situations where my bowels have let go in a very unanticipated way. And it's hellish.

Nonetheless, after I myself found a full adult sized poop on the toilet seat of the patient washroom about a year earlier, I know that sometimes people don't choose wisely, and the end of the story was the same. A shit was in a place that it shouldn't have been. And now someone else had to manage it.

People for sure can be unpredictable, and slightly strange.

This got me thinking about a very fond childhood memory. Fond, because it involved a funny pooh story, that now has enough space and time between the actual event to have blossomed into a hilarious memory. And it got me thinking about how parenting has vastly changed what I hold to high standards and what I absolutely could not give one crap about.

So which side of the fence do you sit on? Have your standards increased with parenting, or have you drifted to that place where just survival exists. The place where you are happy if your children are dressed, eating something that isn't carb related, and not punching one another? The place where arriving at a flushed toilet in your own home, makes you feel like you ARE doing this! You are teaching them life skills!

When I was 8 and my sister 10, we lived on our cul-de-sac in Toronto. One day my sister's friend Erin came over to play in our sprinkler (names changed to protect her identity....well... 'cause....read on). Erin lived in a very very very tidy house. We were not allowed to play in it. The one time I was allowed to stand in the foyer, I could see that the couch and chair in her living room were wrapped in plastic.

I had a tidy and clean house. But nothing wrapped in plastic. Unfortunate orange carpeting in the living room, but clean and bright and fairly fresh smelling. My dad, though lovely, was a hardass rules kind of person. He did not bend for much and took delight in getting frustrated and shouty about the small things.

Erin, my sister, and I were running back and forth through the sprinkler. The grass was sodden as we ran, jumped, slipped and rolled in it, post-sprinkler jump. It was hot out, and that was the 80's way to cool down. No one had a pool. It was run like a lunatic through a sprinkler and drink from the hose, or die from the heat, kind of weather.

About twenty minutes into this and completely soaking wet, Erin announced that she had to poop. This quickly became a huge dilemma as she had to go "really bad" and she knew that she wouldn't be able to pop into her house across the road because of how wet and grass covered she was. She knew with her parents that trying such a thing would land her in enormous trouble.

"Well you can't go into our house then" I piped up in my knowingly very bossy unhelpful way "cause we'll get into trouble too if you get grass all over the floor."

My sister, looking very thoughtful, had a moment to look at Erin who was doing the "I need a shit dance" and said "it's probably okay if you just poop in the yard."

Our backyard was huge, at the bottom of a slight hill, surrounded by bushes. Erin crept off, had her poop, returned, and blissfully continued to run through the sprinkler. We didn't think about it again.

As poor timing would have it for us and Erin, later that night in the cool of the evening, when the grass had all dried, I heard the door slam closed and the familiar sound of an engine starting. My dad had fired up the lawnmower and was out cutting the grass.

He got about 15 minutes into it when the lawnmower sound, ground to a halt. There was silence, and then the front door flung open and my dad shouted in a really angry voice, "Who crapped on our lawn?"

Silence in the house.

"There is a full sized human turd on our lawn and I want to know who did it!"

I heard my sister's timid voice from her bedroom. "It was probably just a big dog dad."

My dad was NOT buying the dog story. He made us come outside to the lawn to look at the MASSIVE poop that Erin had obviously been storing for weeks, right in the middle of the yard. At 8, even I knew that at least shoving your bum into a bush and crapping there, would both deliver the poop somewhere less likely to be seen and cover your bum from any passing neighbors.

Looking at it, it was obvious that one of two things had happened. A human had shit there. Or a horse had somehow found its way into our backyard, in the middle of the city to do its business.

The story ended sadly with a call to Erin's parents, my sister getting grounded for letting someone shit in our yard, and a pretty terrible feeling in our house for the rest of the night.

My dad, who has majorly softened in his years and with whom I am very close, has been chastised by me as an adult for the way he dealt with the shit on the lawn, that hot day in August sometime in the 1980's.

"Like who cares dad. There was a crap on the lawn, why were you so angry and worked up?"

"Well you shouldn't poo on someone's lawn and leave it, and I had to push it into the bush!"

What we agreed upon was that his reaction had not been ideal.

Mine would have been "great, there's a turd. Sigh".

Sometimes I find them unflushed in our house, at least this one would have been surrounded by grass in a summer breeze, in its natural environment. I would have been thankful that no one brought their soggy, grass covered limbs into my house and the bathroom, to drip everywhere and leave grass bunches behind for me to clean up one by one, as I found them, for the rest of my life.

I would have explained that poop is for toilets. But when a toilet isn't possible, that poop is for burying.

It would be a great moment to teach (especially for drunken woods parties in northern Ontario years later), that just because you don't think someone can see you pooping, doesn't mean that someone isn't watching you poop. So be private, cover up, and then dig and bury.

Parenting has made me realize what I can and cannot tolerate. What I am willing to tolerate, and what hill I am willing to die on as it pertains to behaviors and battles around them. I pick my battles carefully. Because it's absolutely exhausting otherwise. And quite frankly, my kids can use less anxiety about my standards in their life.

I know that the best kind of dump is the one that no one finds, no matter where the hiding place might be. Bowels, as it turns out, are unpredictable, and I have long learned not to judge anyone for pooping in the woods.

Just please, my boys, the loves of my life, don't shit in a bin. Even if wrapped kindly for the finder to find.

Someone to help pry poop off of anuses that aren't your own

Trigger: do not read, if the father in your life makes you rage.

I'm sorry if Father's Day is a shit sandwich rolled into a fire bomb of divorce, or just current anger toward a partner or ex. Here in our household, Father's Day is a day to celebrate the way that my husband and I plodded into each othe's life in desperation. And then became parents.

And the way that he became a beautiful human, clipper of all toenails, kisser of all faces, teller of one too many crude jokes about bollocks in a British accent, and a true face of kindness when the boys are breaking down.

He is the better parent, the better person, the one more willing to suck up the tiredness. The last to complain. (Mostly. My complaint ratio is much higher and louder).

It's also a day to remember that he is twice a father.

I am twice a mother and that's all we will ever get.

Just as you get to the cusp of life getting back to normal, longer sleep-in days, fewer anuses to pry poop off that aren't your own. You also descend into the 'holy shit, my boys are growing too quickly, how have I missed it?, why can't they stop growing"? part of the film.

Just as the peace finally hits and consumes you, another switch tips over and you go into high grade panic mom about all the loss and fear that's inevitable.

Why does time move so fast? And so slow. Why can't we be a family, always together forever? Same roof, one always 8, one always 13. Sometimes these thoughts make me lose my mind.

Sometime, somewhere else, my child will be. Living their life. And I might be nowhere near them.

This particularly breaks me as I might suspect myself as the shittier parent, but I am the parent the boys always come to kiss and cuddle.

Sneaking up on my 8 year-old while he was playing his game, I was saddened to know that by 17 (in his exact words) he would only kiss me "for pity" (for FUCKiNG PITY) and that he would long be moved to another country "being a chef."

Father's Day might be a painful one for you. From your own relationship with your father, to the parent who you no longer recognize who is trying to parent with you.

But what Father's Day really means, is that someone was born to you. And him. And has become part of your greatest fears and has made you lose any part of you that once was able to make sane choices about safety.

I hope you had a brilliant day.

Here's to the promise for future pity kisses.

Gosh darn it.

Don't throw it out (but also, don't fucking eat it)

Humor in the chaos.

My husband asked for the vintage fruit loops while staying at my dad's place.

My boys love their Fruit Loops x a zillion.

I had a giggle when I pulled them out.

My dad doesn't throw anything edible out.

He also never ever has gastroenteritis. Never has food poisoning. Doesn't vomit or feel nauseated. I cannot for the life of me figure it out.

That 1969's Pepto Bismol in his cupboard must really really work

D.R. Wright

Relationships: the good, the bad and the festering bloody toe

The story of two nerds (we can replace "Jon" with a pseudonym for the book....still thinking about which name might irk him the most :)

My hubs SF (also known as Silver Fox to me. Ha! Makes him cringe), and I met on a blind date after what seemed like an eternity of chatting on the phone (before online was a thing).

He made me laugh a lot and I was fairly sure a serial killer wouldn't have taken the time to do that, so I took a chance and met him in person.

I asked him what his teeth were like (knowing he was a Brit). He told me he didn't have a Hollywood smile but couldn't eat an apple through a tennis racquet either. I was hooked.

We went for a drink and then onto the cinema (which is the dumbest first date ever).

Jon will tell me later that due to a series of blunders he was already running late for our date, when he smashed something into his toe. Not wanting to be tardy, he shoved his wound into his sock and felt the blood oozing out of his foot mixed in with what he thought was glass. Throughout our entire date he sat wondering when it would soak through his shoe, and when I would scream and run away.

He also made the misguided decision not to bring his glasses. I asked to sit at the back of the theater. We watched the longest, most boring film ever and he couldn't see any of it.

He spent three hours in the dark trying to look like he could see, and willing his blood vessels to congeal. I spent three hours wondering if he had a squinty eye issue and why he kept staring at his foot.

As we met the year before I moved back to Canada, what might have been rushed choices in other circumstances became a proposal in ours, and we decided to speed up Jon's Canadian residency process by getting married at Toronto City Hall.

We had mixed feelings about this. I had never pictured a huge wedding, but I had pictured something with all of my closest friends there. City Hall could hold a limited number of people, and our close family was already coming.

Never mind, we thought, we will have a massive celebration/wedding when we are settled and more financially stable.

I left England rather quickly the day after med school ended to catch the beginning of my residency program at Queens University.

Jon and I hadn't seen each other for nine weeks when he arrived for the "real" wedding of my cousin, the day before our rushed wedding.

Needless to say we had a wedding eve baby, by accident (if you need to picture a stork to make that more palatable, please do).

The next day we met at City Hall.

Our now oldest would be with us, in zygote form only. We would have no idea until 2 months later, while I was in residency and living with a close friend and his wonderful family. Jon was still in England.

I had resigned myself to the fact that I likely had Diabetes from the amount of peeing that I was doing, and the seemingly never ending thirst. My final diagnosis of "pregnancy," although a complete surprise, was a very welcome one.

The day of the wedding arrived. Even though it was a small town hall wedding, the bridal stress was not lessened at all. My parents, who had divorced in a fairly acrimonious way 12 years before, would be seeing each other for the first time since. I was scared. What if our wedding became a war?

Jon's parents were in Canada for the first time. What if they hated Canada? What if they did not approve of their son moving so far away?

Fortunately, the universe decided to be kind on that day.

My mom was well into her horrible neurodegenerative disease journey at that point. My ever classy dad walked over and said "hello, you look beautiful." She said to me "who was that kind man?" They had been married for 25 years. Her dementia, in that moment, was the only kindness her disease brought to us.

City Hall was intimate, beautiful and loving.

We made our vows while Ray LaMontagne crooned in the background.

The ceremony itself was simple and fast and full of love.

In the end we didn't have a huge wedding full of love. We never got financially stable. We had a baby full of love and shit explosions up his back, instead.

Someday we will have that massive celebration.

Until then we celebrate our two children, their health and our continued flaw-filled adventures together.

My chin hair patch.

First world problem time

Scroll past if you are looking for something more relevant OR if you don't want to know a home remedy to remove thick hairs from one's chin.

Please don't scroll past cruelly if you have such a remedy.

So here's the thing. I have this patch of hair on my left chin. I actually think I'd be better serving whatever picture you are making for yourself in your mind, by calling it a tuft. An angry tuft. An angry thick, black and pokey tuft. With one completely sharp and thick white hair in the middle of the pubey black ones. On the right side of my chin, there are also one or two stragglers. They are also thick.

Like the tuft, at any time, they can also grow at the rate of seven meters a minute.

I have asked about these before.

You have helpfully suggested laser treatments. I really don't know if this is still a thing where I live, but between kids, and full time family medicine and Covid, I failed miserably on this suggestion.

You suggested waxing. I did try this on my legs first with the pot of liquid hell, and then with the strips. In the first case, my legs stuck to each other and then to the wall of the shower. Much help was needed from my spouse for weeks to come for this situation. The strips were a bit better, but I didn't find they pulled out all of the hairs, only some. As if to tease me into going back "full pot".

I then got an Epilator. It is my best friend. I love it so much for my legs and my mustache area (even if the latter makes me weep from the pinchy pain). My armpit tore off when I tried it there, and I am at peace with keeping razors for this area. The Epilator is a gift from the gods, however, even with the slit shaped, "let's make it so that you cannot tear off your face" attachment, it does not pull the tufts out.

I am guessing it's because underneath my chin skin, there are barrels of concrete within which the roots of the tuft hairs sit. And some lovely (likely female) dermatologist is about to discover that there are some fibroblasts in the dermis that actually produce concrete, within my chin, on my face.

So this is usually where my last resource comes out.

Tweezers seem to be the only thing that removes these hairs. I use the old "rear view mirror trick" both to get the best light and because I know that these hairs can go from nothing to a full meter in length in the time it takes between last looking in the mirror before starting the car, and when you arrive twenty minutes later at your destination.

We have two sets of reliable tweezers. Both of these have been doing a complete rockstar job on the tuft. Until two days ago.

Two days ago I realized that I could not find either set of tweezers.

I had ignored the panic I was feeling when I realized that one set was gone, and that it was likely related to one of the three boys in the house. Meaning, that I would never find them again. Besides, if boys are picking things out of boy bits, those sets are dead to me anyway.

I kept my other set close, but not close enough apparently. I should have slept with them under my pillow.

Two days ago I asked my husband if he had seen them. He said he had no idea BUT, I also realized that his little wispy, pube-like ear side danglers were all gone.

I looked him straight in the eyes and asked "How? Did? You? Remove? Your? Ear? Hairs?"

He answered nonchalantly "with the tweezers!"

Which tweezers?

A shrug.

I pointed to the tuft on my face. I could see from the look in his eyes that he knew he was responsible for both my current problem and my possible solution.

"But you asked me to tidy the other day and so I did!"

My husband is lovely and incredible and amazing. He does the lion's share of our family's work, but tidying means throwing things into drawers, including empty wrappers, and anything laying anywhere at the time.

He has been known to tidy my underwear into the fish tank drawer and an empty biscuit packet into my bedside table. Every drawer is filled with his "tidiness." Anything that is not animal or human, is tidied into a drawer. I know that when this means finding a pen becomes an "all day task", that retrieving my tweezers is akin to finding a needle in a haystack.

Our apartment has more drawers than the average human to drawer allotment (x ten).

So now, his ears look less "Lord of the Rings", he is feeling sheepish and I have a tuft left and do not know how to manage it.

Everything is on lockdown apart from essentials.

I have ordered two more sets of tweezers from Amazon. They are both brightly colored to hopefully avoid this scenario in the future.

In the meantime, when I go out with my mask on, I am fairly certain the 5 sharp hairs pointing at right angles to my skin will burst through the fabric and break the tight fit between myself and the outer world. I also worry that if the wind is blowing, then the poking facial hair stringy things might confuse a passerby for me having an insect in my mask, and then everything might break loose.

So please, for the love of goodness (with safety at the top of your mind while making your suggestions), how do I remove my facial chin pubes safely? while waiting for everything else to arrive? The Amazon man it seems, who used to live under my sink, has now moved out of the building and can take several days to get anything to me.

Do I ignore it and hope others will do the same? Scrub off any particularly stubborn wall stains with my face and make use of the horror? Hope I can find a strip of wax somewhere and deal with the third degree burns, or do you have another way forward?

Please tell me you have something else? Please!!!!

I promise we aren't stealing anything. Connections made during Covid.

Feel good post for a haggard day! Only read if you enjoy a long ramble!

For everyone worn out by the constant background stress of Coronavirus, I am hoping this will make you smile. I was reminded of the very small but mighty great things that have come out of Coronavirus, when I got home to find a package of baking from "May" (real name kept for privacy).

Let me start by explaining that not only do I live in an apartment (which has been extra stressful with my two kids during lock down), but I live in an apartment that is full of seniors. When I say full, picture the Golden Girls and then picture them again x every single apartment unit in the entire building (minus ONE other young family who lives at the top of the building...we are on the bottom floor).

Working during Corona as a family doctor is stressful enough, especially in the beginning when there are so many unknowns and you are worried that

125

a) your patients might die 'cause you can't examine them over the phone b) you might infect your family from being out and about everyday. But working during a time when you knew that you could take everyone down in your building with you if you got sick, like the Titanic, was the pinnacle of stress.

Our neighbors locked themselves away intensely. What used to be a busy building with the coming and goings of grandchildren quickly became a completely vacant place. People were really scared, and I felt like a threat in my scrubs coming home every day with people peeking out at me from behind curtains with concerned looks. So we were in a bit of a bind when our cat Frosty went missing from the building and we had to figure out how to find her during lockdown.

We had ventured out with our kids on one of the first days that we were allowed to walk around our own neighborhood during lockdown. We felt like complete aliens escaping our building and were so nervous about it that we left our cat out on the balcony for the first time alone, without realizing that we had done so. When we came back she was nowhere to be found, having not gotten the Corona cat memo, she had escaped to finally be free and go out and enjoy her new life.

That was a long night. Our kids were devastated about the loss of their cat, and my oldest was up bright and early, out looking for her on the balcony.

We spotted her far away, two balconies over. Relief was replaced by panic when we realized we had no way of getting her back. We didn't know what to do; we briefly knocked on the door we thought belonged to the balcony, but this was back before masks were available, Corona was in its infancy, and NO ONE was coming to their door.

So we snuck up to the balcony and spent 30 mins trying to lure the cat back over. She was scared and confused. Because it looked like no one was home, and I was getting desperate to get our cat back and stop hovering around someone's apartment, I mounted the plexiglass-covered railing and grabbed our cat. This required climbing on a chair and then an incredibly awkward gymnastic-style jazz hand, holy shit, almost fall dismount on the way back over with a caterwauling cat.

Just as we were climbing back over our own balcony, haggard from what must have looked like the burglary of the century to every occupant peering out of their apartment windows, I heard a voice yell "I hope your cat is okay." The voice came from a tiny, white-haired woman who couldn't hear me scream back, "I'm so sorry, we didn't mean to break onto your balcony, we tried to knock first, my 12 year-old couldn't live without his cat", no matter how hard I shouted.

That night my kids made a card, with our phone number on it, and we had baked a cake for the little elderly woman who we now know as "Aunt

May"*. At that point, as we rang the bell and ran away, we weren't sure that our cellophane-covered cake was okay to leave, so we left a note to wipe it down with alcohol first.

This is what started our 4 month friendship with May. We have seen each other several times from over 100 feet away on our balconies but have never met in person. She has frantically waved at our kids during nights when organized clapping for front line staff happened, and has looked over and smiled sadly when we had a full building vigil, first for the shooting victims (NS) and then for the funeral that went by for the downed Snowbirds pilot.

She has dropped off baking and cards for us, I have brought her alcohol gel (woohoo distilleries), and treats at the shop when I went.

May has texted that we have kept her sane, living alone during a time when her main visitors were usually her own grandchildren, who weren't allowed to come into the building. And she in return has reminded us that kind people, both old and young, are the valuable things that keep life happy, and the stress levels down. I'm hoping one day to meet May in person, but for now, we still revel in leaving packages on her doorstep, ringing the doorbell and running away like the thieves that first snuck onto her balcony.

Stay well everyone.

Gardening: So good, in theory. So shite, in practice.

Anyone else winning in life?

Winning in gardening?

$2 million spent on seeds.

Lugging of bags of soil to our apartment patio.

The torture of the daily reminder to children to water the plants. The fight for who will do it, who was wronged in this decision, and who will be punished the next day with having to carry

A. Single. Pot. Of. Water.

Ten. Feet.

For a bountiful harvest.

Of two cucumbers.

The size of my.

Thumb.

Things that go sting in the night.

What is this hellfire?????? And can it kill me?

When you feel like popping outside, but then an orange stick figure with an extra long tail zaparoo thingy and antennae that look like antlers is there, on the outside.

And it's doing this weird bum grindy thing against the window.

And you notice one of its leggy sticky bits thingies is shaped like a "u".

And it has too many knee joints.

And a blueberry for a thorax.

And you know what sound it will make as it leaves the door, hits your eyelid, and then your arms, as you wave them frantically, and scream and then it hits the window again with a loud "snap".

And you know the sound of your soul dying as you stand in the dark wondering where in the Fack it has landed, and whether or not you can get inside

133

again before it gets you with that half-eaten tip of his black pokey poker..

And when you can start breathing again.

So you stand there and consider this your last thought before the insects take over and you die while on a camping trip, with friends just meters inside, if you decide to go out.

So you stay inside.

Colonoscopy prep: Help me with hellfire

I'm at the transitional stage of colonoscopy prep. Just like in labour, the momentum is barrelling down a river called my bowel. Everything hurts. This came long after the "hey, I'm managing this ok stage", and not far from the, "my anus is literally like a chewed orange" stage. It's all completely out of control now. Like a derailed train. Someone tell me something funny.

Please. I'm weak. I want pizza and someone is going through pre-existing holes into my body with a camera tomorrow. One of those pre-existing gateways being a chewed orange.

I have a ton of Vaseline onboard. I'm doing all the right things.

I just need humour to get me through.

The worst you can do is make me poop myself laughing, and I'm already heading toward that career path without your help.

Jokes. Memes. Anything. Please.

Amazon roulette.

Please please tell me about your best Amazon "roulette" purchase ever.

Amazon can be great if you need clothes desperately (like me, somehow blowing through parts of my underwear), in that they arrive in ten minutes from the man down the hall.

But unless you've ordered the same clothing you already own, you are seriously taking your chances with what might show up.

While my boys were at soccer, I was unpacking my latest packages.

When I opened the amazing Calvin Klein sports bra "lette" I had ordered I was slightly surprised at the size.

I missed the "lette" details when ordering in a fury under my desk at work at the end of the day while fetching a disability tax credit form that had fallen behind my desk (as you do). So I've basically ordered a child's bra that would fit a hamster. Each side holds a single one of my nipples. Which makes it a challenge for doing things.

In another package I got some awesome underwear I'd been hoping for as a replacement. Along with the underwear in the photo below, came five pairs, in all sorts of "I look like I should be buried" colours.

Surprisingly I tried them on for fun. They hold half my body, and I'm enjoying how inviting that feels. The material feels a bit flammable but meh, whatevs!

I'll laugh in public about them and likely end up wearing them every day. I'm certain I didn't order them.

One day I'm hoping I feel as powerful in them as Jack Black does in his Nacho Libre underwear.

They are absolute fire!!!

Thank you Amazon roulette.

Whatcha got that you weren't hoping for (maybe a comfy, sexy surprise like I got)? (also I have to say these aren't far off from my real underwear. What's amazing about them is the waist is like a mile thick....superhero style!)

Gary the turtle

What are you up to to start off the weekend?

So despite being a short week, this was a loooong one in the land of the Family medicine people! Today, especially so. Paper is raining from the sky and finding its way onto my desk for more patients than I knew I had in my practice.

So I asked Jon and the kids to meet me by the lake after work. By the time we got there it was grey and cold. A perfect fall feeling day. Except it's spring. So we were all "end of the week angry" about this kind of shite.

We walked down the forest trail to the lake and were swarmed by Mayflies. Which is especially awesome when you have a lot of hair.

Then we get to the beach and I'm freezing, the sky is grey, the water is really high and there is barely any beach left from the heavy rain we have had this past week. My feet were cold. I'm wearing scrubs and the tiredness is hitting hard.

But the boys persisted; against the wind and on a narrow beach we poked. Boys with net in hand, trying to find a slightly bulbous tadpole (they are MASSIVE here), and me thinking we are going to find nothing because the reedy part of the lake is buried in water.

I told my oldest the other day, as we plodded through the forest, that I quite fancied finding a turtle. I promised him that day that if he found one (knowing he wouldn't), he could have basically anything he wanted. No turtle.

So I was a little skeptical when he ran toward me, at 13, with his cool 13 year-old saunter, and a net in his hands, saying he caught a turtle. Especially since the net was tiny and the thing inside was the size of an avocado pit.

Nonetheless he rescued a half-dead, belly up, itty-bitty lad of a guy we called Gary. So we did our version of turtle CPR, gave him a long talk about resilience, put him somewhere safe and watched him plod off toward the water. Gary, as it turned out, had life in him yet.

As a small snapping turtle I hope that Gary remembers us with kindness later in the summer when we are swimming in the same lake and step on him or a family member as big, stompy boy-feet tend to do.

Then we found the chonkiest tadpole ever. We hung around with him for a bit while he checked out our bucket, then we wished him well and off he went.

With tail and bulb body he pushed his way through the water, hopefully growing legs and arms soon, to be caught by us again later this summer in his frog body.

It turned out to be an excellent end to our evening. Despite my cold misery and feeling annoyed that the sky looked like it was threatening snow.

As we were walking back to the car we were swarmed by mosquitos (we meaning me, 'cause they love hair), and one went right up my nostril at an alarming and shocking speed.

It has yet to come out that I have seen. Despite me doing an emergency pick because I panicked, during the frenzy of "having an insect as part of my face". My youngest immediately told me off (despite an obvious life threatening object torpedoing through my nasal passages). At seven, and doing the disgusting things he does almost hourly, I would have thought he could have given me a break.

So likely I will die of west nile or of a mosquito boring into my sinuses and then having babies, as they do.

Nonetheless. Happy Friday.

Prayers for Gary, the size of my thumb, who will likely get eaten by a bird tomorrow but who brought much joy to our lives tonight.

Glad the weekend is here.

The time my spine said "nope".

I'm sharing this in the hopes of helping to save you from yourself.

If you are anything like me, you will need the heads up.

I hope for your sake you are not.

This morning I woke up to a positive message on a friend's facebook page.

Something about "perspective" and "goals" and the ability to start again at any time. To seize the day. To grab life as you can!

I am 44, with two kids and am in family medicine. Since Covid has hit, our tiny apartment gym has closed.

I have eaten my way through many exceptionally tasty emotions and I am not quite in the shape I was in a few years ago. Ahem, okay maybe 20 years ago.

145

I had also booked today off a couple of months ago (the way you have to book time off in family medicine) to have a day to MYSELF.

To lay on the couch, in the fetal position, possibly making moaning sounds, and watching something like Grey's Anatomy, the Crown, or Dead To Me over and over again while eating enormous amounts of something. I have not had a day off without kids since Covid started. Not a single day. Today (and yesterday) were supposed to be the days.

I also have an enormous amount of paperwork to catch up on….but I was thinking "who cares", I will be on the couch, alone, and no one will be poking me, or calling my name and I will be patient-visit free, and all will be glorious. And I can poop by myself, should I choose to do so.

As it turns out, my one child is home as his school had a Covid exposure and they need an entire week to clean.

And my other child is home for a PD day.

So, when I woke up this morning to that message from my friend's facebook page, my first thought was eff-off. My feeling sorry for myself meter was running HIGH.

But then I laid there thinking about it. And with a purring cat on my head I decided to seize the day.

Here's where the warning comes in.

In a past lifetime, I was a paramedic. You had to train quite hard to pass the physical part of the job when applying in Toronto, and I used to be, what I thought, was really quite strong. In effect you would spend the day lifting really heavy objects over and over.

I also used to really enjoy gymnastics.

Living in a small apartment, with no outdoor space, you wouldn't think that gymnastics was possibly the most obvious thought to have to start my downtrodden, kid-filled, supposed to be 'first solo day off' since March, day. But well......

Here's where the warning comes in again.

The thing is, our boys are obsessed with Kobra Kai. And when you are stuck watching something over and over like that, you sort of feel like trying out the moves yourself. I had flirted with a couple of kicks last night. One was even higher than I thought my leg could ever go again.

They went okay. I can't move my one leg entirely normally this morning, but it did feel really good at the time. I felt like my powerful self was back.

So this morning, I decided to say eff you to the universe, push back the parts of me that were feeling sorry for myself, and attempt a handstand.

There are several reasons why I chose this, which I won't go into at the moment.

But I had surprised myself at a friend's cottage this summer by doing a few to "show all of the kids" how to do them, and hadn't let myself down entirely.

I was feeling ready for my powerful self to make a move, stick it to Covid, and seize the day, like my friend's facebook post told me I could.

So I did a handstand against the wall.

For a split second I felt AWESOME. Like totally powerful.

Then I didn't.

Because a handstand against the wall is different than a handstand on free ground.

Outside on the grass, the gravity brought me down any which way I wobbled.

Against the wall, my legs were leaning further over my head, beyond what gravity would have allowed outside.

And I got stuck.

But don't worry, my panic only lasted for a millisecond....

Before my right arm gave out (which was surprising as that is my dominant arm).

Since I had no way to get my legs back over my head, and my right arm had collapsed at the elbow, I basically melted down the wall.

It was not a smooth "melt", as the word melt would leave you to believe, but rather a "thud" melt; a combination of my shoulder hitting the ground and my ego leaving my body.

Here's another warning. The human neck does not like to be at complete right angles to the human shoulder.

I finished the hand stand in the only way that could be done when one has no upper body strength and no control of their legs; with a massive slide onto the ground, head first, arms splayed, the transverse processes of my spine becoming one with our wall molding. It took mere milliseconds, but I felt like my whole life had been laid out before me.

I'm not sure what the lesson is here.

I'm not ready to give up on my strength or my dreams of being a gymnast again.

The reality of parenting while trying to relax and chart has hit like a thud, as has my body trying to do a handstand.

Stay safe everyone. Keep on trying to win at life.

D.R. Wright

Swings. Don't be fooled by how great they look (aka tires over lakes are tricky bastards)

For those of you who could touch your toes but now cannot due to the weight you have put on with Covid, this story is for you. Beware. Those extra pounds give a new centre of gravity and a whole new dimension to bending.

For those of you who need a laugh or perhaps a warning about your physical abilities during Covid; this one's for you.

Trigger warning: getting stuck in a tire over a body of water

So yesterday was my paperwork day. Out of the clinic, and after staring at my computer for five hours (and with the heaviness of everything looming from the day before), I decided to head out for a walk.

I encouraged my family to come (well, not really so much encouraged as much as made it sound like a really really long walk), and high fived myself as everyone said they were happy to stay put and hang out.

I decided to go for a jaunt to the woods, which is my sane place at all times (but particularly these times), and picked a place that I've been meaning to go to for a while. It was a bit of a jaunt, but pre-Covid I had been at the gym every day, so when Jon texted (sometimes I get a bit lost), I smugly sent him the photo below...I was not only great, but was cleverly finally making a move to get back in shape after all the Covid eating and sitting I've been doing.

I'd been meaning to go to the place I was headed to because of this amazing tire swing that hangs over a lake that I can see from the road every day as I drive by. So with my 'mom' jeans on (flexible elastic waistband), and Bob Seger blasting in my ears, I really felt I knew what I had to do.

Five minutes later I was in the tire hanging above the lake. It was beautiful out and I felt lucky to be alive with the sun shining on my face and no one around. I felt a bit off balance but then some Neil Diamond came on and I thought, probably I could take on the world at that point.

And then I looked back. This is the moment I realized two things. One, the ten pounds I've gained since Covid started had in fact become an agility hazard, and two, from how far the swing was now out from its position of origin, I could see this is why I had never seen anyone on it.

I panicked a bit then remembered I had at one point had two human heads come out of my body and that dismounting from a swing was likely not comparable in the category of "hardness".

And that's when the actual "in-shape" mom (who clearly has been exercising since the start of the pandemic) and her daughter showed up on their bikes. And her daughter wanted to "try the swing", as soon as I was done.

What I wanted to say was "you can't try the swing, social distancing means that you shouldn't be touching anything a stranger has just touched" (which I realized meant I shouldn't have been on it either),...but what I said instead was "ok I'll get right off."

The conclusion to this story was that there was no "just getting right off."

If you picture an octopus trying to get out of a wet paper bag, that was the start of my dismount. Now flip the bag upside down and hit fast forward on your remote. I didn't fall in the water as the tire flipped over, but my upper body strength let me down enough to have me hanging by one arm as the tire swung back and bumped me into the shore.

The mom's gasp and her running toward me while I yelled out "no! Keep six feet away, I'm fine", in slow motion added to the coolness I felt.

I will not be re-attempting that tire anytime soon.

If you feel you can physically do what you did pre-covid right now, you might want to do a little tester beforehand, before trying something more complicated. Just sayin'.

Spiders. How can something so small be so powerful (to my nervous system and my armpit glands)?

Trigger warning: Spiders

On the back of what's below, does anyone have any good ideas for dock spiders, to make them less part of a cottagers day to day lives, other than leaving them alone? Has anyone ever been bitten?

So when faced with a potentially life threatening situation, my brain goes automatically to figuring out as much as I can about this situation (ie what I did for days and days and hours and hours, after Covid hit, to try and protect my patients, my family and myself).

So when my best friend and I were minding our own business, sitting on a Canadian dock, talking about 44 year-old mom things while our children played Sardines in the woods, and a dock spider popped up onto the dock, I figured the best defense is a good offense. So tonight, upon

155

returning to suburbia, I did some reading and I did NOT like what I found out about Canada's largest spider.

Let me paint a picture for you first. My friend and I are harmless. We might be slightly inappropriate at times, wear mom clothes and lounge around forever talking about our twenties, but we are harmless creatures and would appear so to most living beings as well. We were sitting minding our own business when something with eight legs that looked like my dad's legs (ultra hairy and thick...and I mean the exact same size), came cruising across the dock.

My friend, being the ever more hardcore of the two of us, nonchalantly walked down to the dock to give the wood a bit of a stomp, hoping to send the spider back under the dock, allowing us to live in peaceful and blissful ignorance of what lives around us once again.

The spider, which was roughly the size of my friend's head, saw her coming and lunged off the dock into the water. I remembered that dock spiders could swim a bit, from my long days of shrieking at dock spiders crawling out of my canoe as a child (and then attaching their web-thingy stringy-thingy to the side of my canoe, as I flung them over and feared for my life.....don't feel sorry for them, they took it as a challenge and water-skied behind the canoe no matter how fast I paddled; picture

Weekend at Bernies, but with Bernie alive, wearing a spider costume...and also being Satan).

But this spider pretty much grabbed his snorkel gear and fins and RAN across the water (spider Jesus looks NOTHING like real Jesus by the way, so don't be fooled by this trickery)!

He then, after what would have been the swimming challenge of my life, climbed up the vertical side of a massive rock without wavering and turned around with a gaze that said he gave zero shits that his life could be in danger from the height or the drop from it.

We then watched said spider, with his hairy thick body try to catch DISH and I from the side of a rock. He needed zero rest, while he effortlessly somehow half dangled into the water with his poisonous dangly-bit thingies while hanging from the side of a rock!

Here's what I found out about these fascinating, horrific souls.

They can stay underwater for 30 minutes!!

They are unsquashable (imagine trying to squish Grandpa's leg with a very small shoe) and they run like Ben Johnson!

They fish! They don't catch their prey with a web- although they weave webs to carry around their THOUSAND spider eggs and make a web to act as a playpen for their THOUSAND babies.

They have waterproof legs that let them run on top of the water- they can jump vertically to keep from being eaten by fish.

They eat insects, tadpoles and fish!!!!! (well minnows, but STILL!)

They are hairier than my legs in the winter. Which is saying a lot. Like a lot!

The male only reproduces once- after releasing it's sperm, it sticks to the female and then dies AND she eats him for nourishment (insert horror face, and then smirking face here)!

Let's face it, they should be Canada's National Animal (even though they are not an animal), as they will never ever be extinct and therefore will always represent!

Every single Canadian cottage has about several million that live on the underside of the dock.

They WILL sneak onto you just to have a laugh!

They give zero shits about anything.

The wheel of helplessness

Hoping to save someone's life.

Or elbows. Knee caps. Or self-esteem.

Covid has not been kind to my emotional eating habits. Take away the gym and my social habits with close friends and all I have left is the shovelling of Cadbury bars toward my mouth. Non-stop. X 12 months.

I am now in a much better place. Not that Covid is less stressful ('cause family practice during Covid feels like when you stick on a pantyliner and the adhesive gets stuck to your labia right away instead....it continues to be that painful), it's just that I've decided that I can no longer feel so bad from all of the bad coping skills I've acquired.

So onward and upward. More water, more movement, more mindful eating...here I go.

So in a fantastic frenzy of New Year's body resolutions, I found and purchased this wheel.

"Help your abs grow stronger" it says, "increase your arm strength."

What it doesn't say is that you need a bit of strength in both areas before you use it.

How do you know if you have either? Well...I think it was a good measure of arm strength when I tried to get out of a pool while in the middle of strangers two summers ago and couldn't pull myself out.

Despite trying to bob up nonchalantly first.

And having some small child watching me the whole time, then having to pretend I was doing a funky dance move at the side of the pool. While smiling broadly on the outside (crying heartily on the inside). The knowingly disappointed look on the child's face while watching me intently, said it all really.

I knew I had no ab muscles when I tried to do a sit up and popped something in my neck instead.

Still. The shiny box made promises. And the price was right.

It comes double wheeled for "stability." Which was reassuring as after trying the hand stand, I know my stability isn't my strong point.

But, after being forced to take physics in university and never knowing why, it finally came in handy, realizing that past a certain point, your force will move the wheel forward no matter how much you wish the wheel would stop.

So. If you don't have arm strength and are a bit shy on abdominal strength you should hold off on the wheel that promises arm strength and abdominal strength.

Because otherwise the course of events is as follows.

You position yourself like a boss on the floor, after fixing the hand grips to the wheel uses up most of your will to live.

You look at the instructions and memorize the proper technique.

You grasp the wheel handles tightly, and slowly ease yourself forward feeling so badass that "yes you are doing this"!!!

The double wheel feels sturdy as hell. Your inner queen starts to shine.

You feel a pull in the region that must be your abs.

The wheel inches forward slowly. Your arms tighten and you feel something starting to burn. The burning is your muscles' last feeling before they die.

The wheel inches forward with more enthusiasm, almost as if you don't have control of it.

You don't have control of it.

The wheel moves at lightning speed, your right elbow makes the sound you last heard when opening a bag of chips as it hits the ground.

Your lower back becomes separate from one of your vertebrae.

Something underneath you bounces and in slow motion makes first a sticking, and then a strange recoil sound. That something is your skin.

Your kneecaps dig into the ground in a way you have neither agreed upon, nor imaged was physically possible.

Your glasses fly off.

Your child shouts gleefully "look at mommy she fell over!"

Your hair is a bit caught in the wheel.

Your soul dies.

You try it again, convinced that what just happened wasn't in the brochure.

And.

You.

Repeat the steps above.

All of them.

Save yourself from the wheel of hell.

Do some push ups and sit ups and may the force be with you.

Being the child of a medical professional is sometimes harmful to your health

I had just spent the week ordering investigations any time anything remotely worrying came through the door. If a patient had abdominal pain, I would order an ultrasound, blood work and maybe a Cat Scan (big tube-y thing that you lay in. Takes images of your body parts). If someone felt tired, a panel of investigations ordered after a head to toe exam. If someone was farting more than usual I would make sure everything was completely ruled out before declaring it the problem of too much fibre, or too many carbohydrates. I was in my first year in practice, in the deep end fully, forgetting that my clinical insight and previous experience needn't have me rely on 'all of the testing all of the time.' People in healthcare finances were likely making tutting noises a lot to themselves, but I was just doing my best to be thorough. Compelled by anxiety not to let anything fall through the cracks, my ordering was well justified in my "fresh out of the medical residency program bag" brain. Pretty normal for a first year in practice (I happily told myself).

From "my toenail feels funny" to "my bum itches every few months", my radar was still set to fire at any low level of suspicion. The hematologists must have loved me as a new grad. Any abnormality in a CBC would herald a referral to them.[3] They must have thought, "there's always one who slips through the cracks in medical school." I was a one-doctor ordering machine and nothing was getting past me. Every abnormal test looked at with a microscope, every symptom something to take very seriously. Many nights I pondered if I had missed something, making a mental note to bring a patient in again to re-review their symptoms and re-do their examination.

And maybe again.

That much over-investigation and follow up is exhausting, and my time off with my family meant everything.

One Saturday I was enjoying some free time in our backyard with my youngest (let's call him

---

[3] A CBC is a Complete blood count. This can tell us a lot about what might be going on in your body. But usually when one or two points off, as a single snapshot in time, means absolutely diddly squat.

"Foots", aged 3), and the Silver Fox (my husband-but with way less Silver).[4]

"Mummy there's a buzz buzz in my ear."

I rolled over from my position on the grass, grabbed my stout three-year-old and pulled him into a cuddle. "Oh yeah?" I said, "tell me more."

"It's tickly and then it's not."

I'm thinking about all of the times that my ear 'goes off': randomly in the middle of the night; while talking to patients; while in the shower. A small screeching that sounds like a little "wheeeeeeeeee" that comes and goes as it pleases. It doesn't sound like what my patients describe as tinnitus (ie ringing in the ear). Just a small annoying zappy whistley thingy every once in a while. Like your TV when all of those stripey colours come up, and something is being re-programmed[5].

With my hearing being super sharp (if you are a child within two blocks of me and up to something bad or disgusting, I will hear you. If you

---

[4] My two boys, I've named Foots (lover of football and extremely crafty feet), Birdie (his actual nickname being another animal altogether in real life) and SF is my husband, "Silver Fox", a dignified combination of a sexy accent and gray coloured hair. This is to give them some anonymity in the world of my storytelling.

[5] If you're not old enough to remember the tv lines that appeared with a grossly offensive sound, then enjoy your knee joints while they still move properly at all times of the day.

chew with your mouth open, you are dead to me), and it having occurred on and off for years, I was pretty sure that nothing bad was happening in my own ear, and then by extension in the ear of my son.

I smell his delicious warm hair, give him a cuddle and then lift him off, offer a small pat on the bum to get him running through grass again. "I'm sure it's just fine, buddy."

Throughout the day "Mom, my ear went buzzaroo."

Or "It's in there, the buzzy bit."

Every time, I gently encourage him to ignore it.

"Don't worry bub, our bodies make noises all of the time. Does it hurt?"

"Nope, it's just a bit of a buzzy noise."

He is being easily distracted from it, and I think that means it's probably not much of anything.

That night while in the bath playing with cars, sinking them one after the other into the deep bubbles, I hear, "My ear did a crawly."

Feeling his forehead gently, checking his nose for green globs. No cough yet. Eating well.

I do a quick sneak of the rest of his skin. No rashes.

I watch him as he looks down to grab his cars without pain. No neck stiffness.

I wonder if there's a piece of wax or if this is the start of an ear infection.

I know that only time will tell. If it's going to be something, it will present itself.

I start to think about how I will stay home from work if SF somehow cannot take time off from his own job and Foots becomes sick. Pondering how I will cancel all of my patients and where I will reschedule them in the following days (my schedule is already overflowing weeks in advance).

Then we are lying in bed, stroking the hair of our sweet three year-old sweat pig, the heat from his body radiating off as it always does as he falls asleep. Soother in mouth, sucking to a rhythm then stopping, as his eyes under eyelids wander back and forth, and he is almost out for the night.

Stroking his hair. Chatting with SF. Almost at the point when we gently carry him to his own room, for the hope of a night full of sleep (spoiler: that never happened).

Then a small move of his head. A gentle moment at the start of a dream. And a black thing rolls out from the ear he has been complaining about.

A flying ant. A dead flying ant.

I nudge SF gently, as he is oblivious to all things: People running by naked, a dog without hair, an insect rolling in the fetal position out of his son's ear.

"What in the bloody hell?" he whispers.

I gently pick up the carcass of my son's ear terrorizer. Check the body. Wings and crawly things intact. I tiptoe out, missing the creaky floorboard. Into the toilet it goes.

"My ear is zappyroo," I hear him say earlier. Yes honey. And your mom is an asshole. My medical overchecking apparently is not applicable to my own family.

I silently make note, to book myself in to see my own doctor, to make sure my own ear zap isn't a spider that's been living in my ear canal for the last eight or so years. I head to bed wondering how I can be so great at my job but so crap in my own life.

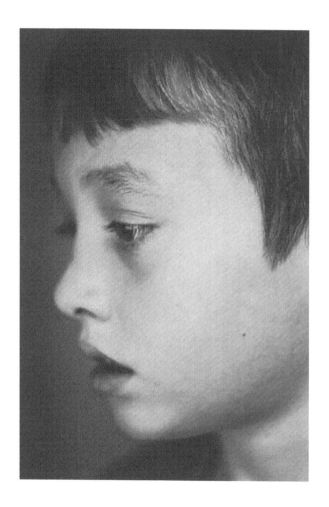

D.R. Wright

I can promise you it's not cancer - the words we live to give.

The heart of medicine is full of great complexity.

If you're not a frequent user of the system then you might picture seeing your doctor once or twice a year for acute things only.

A broken toe
A sore throat.
A refill of contraceptives.
An itchy rash.

But the more we learn about medicine the more complex it has become. There's an entire world of preventative care, trying to help people avoid things like diabetes and the ramifications of such things as chronically high blood pressure, before they become an issue.

Stopping the small steps of wear and tear from becoming the big marks of illness.

Trying to cut down the risk of things like heart attacks and strokes while monitoring for the type of cancers that are both common and treatable if picked up early on screening.

Chronic illness is another thing entirely. The same person is often saddled with many issues.

An overlap of things happening to them physically, posing a risk on their mental wellbeing. Or their mental wellbeing driving them to a place of action or inaction; chemicals and habits that make the body less well or outright sick.

The day is often full of such complexity. A blood pressure and blood work review for someone just discharged from having a heart attack. And anxiety, the type that comes when you start to prepare to see your god a little sooner than expected, in the sheets of the hospital bedding, and a new awful diagnosis.

A patient who has given birth, having trouble not only getting her milk to come in and her infant to latch, but sadly lamenting the fact that her mother's death a year before, means her child will never be held by the arms that the patient felt keenly herself her entire childhood.

An ulcer on a leg, lasting a year in a patient with diabetes who had lost her job during Covid. Whose family had long abandoned her for her "poor choices." Very little money for healthy food.

But worrying most about when that ulcer would actually heal, her daily visits from home health services keeping her emotionally alive.

The toll of it all is heavy for both sides.

The arrangements to keep patients afloat on a sinking ship are complex, and often are far from the mark.

So when a day full of such complexities is scheduled with one or two "quick fixes" slotted in there, I think it's fair to say we all do a happy dance. Being able to use the quick and dirty medical skills from our training is what many of us pictured medicine to be when we signed up for all of those years of schooling.

Doing something practical, that ends in something meaningful and positive.

A problem and a fix.

Yes yes, we love a good long medical mystery that flexes our brain muscles, and enables us to put all of those years of cramming to good use.

But the "quick" in a day full of "messy", is such a relief to see.

Quick assessments, easy treatments, massive relief. Reassurance given easily.

My heart is overjoyed when I see "UTI" in my schedule.[6]

If it's a true urinary tract infection I can sort it out quickly, providing immense relief to the sufferer.

Strep throat.

A quick exam of a throat and respiratory system, a swift swab, a set of vitals and making sure a head can forward flex without stiffness[7] means I can reassure this patient that the treatment plan I am about to give them, will make them feel better really quickly.

So easy to fix. So satisfying.

And with the most precious of all things, "time" given back to focus on the more complex.

Mrs. Richardson booked in for an "urgent same day appointment" for "concerns."

When I brought her in from the waiting room, her face was nervous, her voice rushed and panicked.

---

[6] UTI- urinary tract infection. When bacteria gets into your bladder and makes it super angry, and then peeing becomes miserable. Can also in some instances, travel up to your kidneys and land you in the hospital.

[7] the easy forward bend of the neck often can help to reassure us that we are not currently looking at a severe case of meningitis

Her 80-year-old body convinced she had cancer.

Peeing all the time for the last two days, she spoke with her neighbour who said those were his first signs of cancer. She had also felt a fullness in her pelvis, a slight pain in her back and was a bit tired and under the weather.

Within the two days between her symptoms and her seated in my chair, she and her octogenarian neighbor had not only diagnosed her with cancer, but which kind, and how long she must have left to live.

I was able to sit her down, my hands in her hands and tell her calmly "Mrs. Richardson, you do not have that type of cancer."

"But how do you know?" she blurted out while sobbing.

"Mrs Richardson, you don't have a prostate."

"Prostate cancer therefore, can only happen in men. From your urine dip however, it seems that your two days of extra peeing is from a urinary tract infection."

I've never seen someone have such a perfect cross of confusion and relief at the same time.

"Well I never!!!!" she said looking slightly embarrassed.

"Don't worry", I said, "that's why we are here."

She hugged me and let me know she would let her neighbor's wife know, too. Apparently she had also booked herself with her own family doctor for urgent prostate screening.

Archie, who was profoundly hard of seeing, and his wife, profoundly hard of hearing, were both my patients.

Together they got by, and one was never far from the other. Shouting at him down the hallway as they walked to our room, she looped his arm on mine so I could continue to guide him.

"I'm going to the shop next door to get a few things."

"Don't be long!" he shouted.

"Huh?" she said. While she turned around and muttered "oh never mind", heading to the pharmacy beside us.

"Don't worry Archie. I'll help you find her when we're done."

Archie too, was in a fair bit of panic. After his grandchildren's visit ended the day before, he noticed a large black dot on his arm. He assumed it had been quickly growing as he had never noticed it before. "My dad had a melanoma, I bet to juniper that's what it is and I'll have to lose my arm or something."

I took a look at Archie's arm, looked him in the eye and said "Archie, that's not a melanoma."

"How can you be so sure?"

"What were you doing with your grandchildren yesterday?"

"Oh I don't know, their mother brought stuff to stick and glue to papers. Crafty kind of stuff to keep them busy while we visited."

I picked off the lesion, brought it close to Archie's eyes, which were doing their best squinty impression of trying to see.

"Archie, the only thing you grew was a sequin. Diagnosis: needing to wash your arm more often."

With a chuckle and a soft slug to my arm and saying "phew oh thanks so much doc", I took a four foot tall Archie back to the waiting room to tell his wife, who couldn't hear him, that I'd saved his life.

Small wins.

And a black sequin shoved into my drawer, in case I needed it one day.

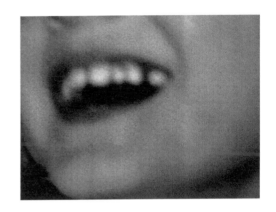

The Final Sprint

Some people (also known as everyone), are not ok.

All essential workers holding together this shit show in whatever form that might be (cleaners, drive-through workers, teachers, docs, nurses, paramedics, etc etc etc). They likely have had their moments of severe fear over personal safety and huge moments of crisis over their family's safety. They are also tired. Keeping that level of fear back constantly in order to function is exhausting.

Wearing a mask all day and breathing your own horridness is also exhausting.

The people stuck at home watching this go down. They are not ok. They are stuck in a situation that is not ideal for a human brain to thrive. Often with children who are a) making them nuts through no fault of their own b) have little access to the natural world and social interaction that they need to thrive.

If you are feeling like you can't hold it together, that is a reasonable feeling. Please connect with someone who can help you hold on until the usual mechanisms that make life comfortable and happy again can kick back into place. Health care is an option for this type of support. There are lots of online options. You are not alone, you are not failing.

If people in your life are appearing to be non-empathetic, extra short tempered, and like they are losing the ability to make rational choices, it's because they have been living in 'fight and flight' mode for too long and are burning out.

If someone cries because the toilet wasn't flushed, the cupboard was left open, or is losing their mind because you forgot to pick up their favorite bread, they are either an a-hole and have always been like this, or are failing to cope during a pandemic.

It has nothing to do with you personally. Please repeat that to yourself ad nauseum throughout the day.

I feel like we are in the final sprint of a very long road race. Picture someone who's breathing heavily, waving their arms frantically in a pair of running shorts and t-shirt that would have fit a year ago, but now appear made for a child. They have lost a shoe, have massive pit stains and have had to poop while running (and didn't stop), hurdling themselves toward the finish line by doing very slow somersaults.

That is everyone.

There is likely still a very very steep hill to climb but the fluorescent sticky line finish tape is in sight.

Finally.

Vaccinations into arms. Follow your local Covid mandates.

If you lash out and say something stupid, that's reasonable. It's also reasonable to apologize, and move on in kindness. If someone apologizes it's reasonable to accept and move on, even if you don't believe it, only to keep yourself floating on whatever positive energy is left.

And if nothing else is left. Then inappropriate humour. And Biscoff Butter. Nutella is also a valid option. Pouring a bag of sugar into your mouth is messier and less satisfying.

Exercise and sleep might be better options.

Check on your outdoor shoes, they are not ok!

Check on your loved ones, they might not be either.

Much love,

Dr Wright.

P.S. This is my ode to Ontario, Canada, as Covid shit hit the fan. Now Covid has hit everywhere.

Unsure if this is appropriate or annoying or what, but family docs are in the land of mental health crisis (patients and ourselves). I have the politically correct version of this conversation a bizillion times a week with patients (obviously with a mental health care plan at the end). They do not see my inappropriate memes, the things that keep me sane in a "dark humour" sort of way in my own personal life (hey, we all need a way through). Writing is a major stress reliever for me. Hoping it will help anyone failing to cope at times or dealing with horrendous people in their personal lives.

P.P.S. I'm going to suggest you take my knowledge with a grain of salt. Coming from a 44 year-old family doc, who has emotionally eaten herself into an extra 40 pounds this year during Covid and has cried several times at things like 'a sticky spot on the floor', ' hitting my foot on the bedpost too hard' or 'the Nutella jar is empty but has been left on the cupboard shelf to taunt me', at the end of a long day of work).

My Final thoughts on Family Medicine.

The last words until we meet again.

What you might not know about your family doctor is that you, as our patients, become weaved into the essence of our daily work and home life.

Your stories and worries, and happiness and fears, become what our lives work purpose is about.

We wish well for you. And when you fall, we hope we provide you the help to get back up yourself. Or that we can carry you until you make it on your own.

At night while making dinner (microwave… let's keep this real), as we glance at our son smiling across the room, we might in that moment think about your son too. How he shines in a different way, how your son's struggles are some I see in my own home. And how I hope, in the end he will find his way again.

When my husband flips me the bird and then smiles in a naughty way, your grandmother's eyes play before mine. Her saucy saucy ways. The way she swears 'cause she knows it will bring out a reaction in me. And because mostly, she doesn't get those reactions anymore. I see her loneliness in the eyes of my son, as he navigates life being a teen.

So in each story you give us. Each secret we keep for you. Each plan we build together to keep you happy and well and safe, there is the heaviness of impending failure. What if we let you down, what if treatments don't work. What if there's nothing left to do. What if you don't choose the path I would for you?

And this weaved narrative from all of these souls we see becomes like a blanket we carry. Working toward keeping us all warm and well sheltered. But often, so so heavy to carry.

And when you pass. We feel thankful that every lesson you shared, every time you made us a better practitioner and every secret you gave to us to hold, remains in ourselves to gift on through care to the next patient.

You live on in many people when you pass.

To my patients, I am one of them. Thank you for trusting me with your body and mind.

To the passing of someone I was growing to know. I hope you soar through your next journey.

Epilogue

Thank you so much for supporting another mom in living her dreams. Mine are: to mom, write and practice medicine well.

Please know that nothing is more important than the comfort of my patients, knowing that they can tell me anything and that their information is completely safe. Always.

Our professional relationship is a legally binding contract of confidentiality.

To this end, not only have all names, dates, personal information and clinical data been changed, but they have been warped such that no particular story is actually about any real patient.

These stories all come from real experiences, but are so completely changed that if you find yourself in one, it's either because the experience you've read about is incredibly common, or you are the embodiment of many of my experiences put together. What you are reading is not about you. Just as it is really about no one in particular.

That old adage about giving chimpanzees a bunch of typewriters and the probability that over time they will type something already written applies here.[8]

All to say, that if you find yourself in one of my stories, this is a coincidence and completely unintentional

This project has hopefully been a stepping stone in "buying more time off" to have a chance to finish a book I started and stupidly thought I could finish in a couple of months. Both funny (I hope) and insightful, this longer collection will let you see what practicing "Cradle to Grave" medicine has been like for me.

Though humour is obviously the way I roll in a lot of spheres of my life (and it gives me great pleasure to bring this into my practice), medicine can be extremely heavy and dark and hard, and unfair.

I am hoping to get my thoughts together enough to give you an insight into it all. The funny and absurd and the heavier pieces of practice. Life is full of both. My hope for you is more large shits on the lawn, and less of the hard suffering.

May you have someone great to medically walk through your journey with you.

---

[8] https://en.wikipedia.org/wiki/Infinite_monkey_theorem#:~:text=The%20infinite%20monkey%20theorem%20states,an%20infinite%20number%20of%20times.

Here is a tiny teaser to the full book
I am writing about Family Medicine.
Hope to see it in your hands one day!

Cancer

It's my last day on a surgical rotation.

I have no idea why there are so many of us, but it seems like a herd of learners has gathered for this morning's rounds.

We have stopped to see a palliative patient. A consult was put in to see if surgery can help with any of her symptoms.

The goal is comfort right until the end.

I am standing in the back of the group. It's been an intensely busy rotation and I am exhausted. I have no talent or drive for surgery and I know I won't be operating on this patient. Still my to-do book is open, ready to frantically record whatever the orders for this patient might be.

As family medicine residents on a surgical rotation we are there to learn, but really the unspoken rule is that we are there to keep patients alive on wards, so that the people who want to be surgeons can be in the operating room operating.

Our Staff Attending (the lead physician responsible for the whole team of junior doctors) starts talking and I look up above the other heads to see our patient. The way I remember it, she is facing the door and is raised slightly up in her bed. Neither of these things make sense but trauma does this to a brain.

Your brain takes what it can cope with and stores it in a way it can remember. And then reforms the information and presents it in a way you might be able to tolerate.

Or sometimes, in the only way it has left.

The patient looks to be in her 30's. But it's hard to tell. Cancer robs people of so many things.

At the end, their life.

Along the way, every day functions, and energy, and sometimes if particularly cruel, part of their brain function.

Even the subcutaneous fat that holds together a facial frame.

Age can become meaningless. Time hanging from bones that no longer look the way that they should.

A face wasting away at thirty-three can look fifty. The image is just as horrible as the reality.

This patient was dying of cancer. I have no memory of what type it was, but I can guess from my recollection of her face and her frame, that we saw it at its most aggressive time.

The stage when family members are told days to weeks left. Maybe if unlucky, hours.

The stage where people stay close to the phone. When pre-covid, as many people who could be there, would make their last visits. Say their final goodbyes.

I am standing looking at her. Feeling like we are imposing on her privacy as is almost always the case in medicine and is a necessary evil in a teaching hospital when herds of learners like ours make privacy an impossibility when rounding in such numbers.

Her eyes are wide, but very glossy, and she appears incredibly weak and thin. I feel like I am watching something that I am not supposed to see. An intimate part of her story not written for my eyes. A breakdown of the body that only the closest to her should know.

So I train my eyes elsewhere, and almost wish I hadn't.

Beside her is a picture of a woman. Well and happy. With a little girl who can't be more than a year old. She is standing beside a man in his 30's who is staring at her with a huge smile on his face.

Three people. Two. Who presumably made another.

Together in a time of happiness.

There is something about the photo that is jarring to me. And I can't stop staring at it, knowing there is something oddly familiar about both adults in the frame.

I look back at the patient. She is struggling to say something. A whisper out of her mouth.

"Sorry?" Says the head resident. Who then shushes everyone while she licks her lips and painfully tries to get the words out again.

I cannot hear what she says.

My mind wanders again to the photo.

Bright eyes, altogether. A family full of life. I look back at the patient. I wonder how she knows these three people in the photo. Wonder if she is related. The eyes seem vaguely similar. No brightness though and with a very sad longing.

My mind is turning. I have a very bad feeling. I put it down to the discomfort of making this woman use part of her last energy reserves talking to us when the surgical consult was clearly futile. But there's something niggling at me the way you feel when you get butterflies in your stomach and sense you've done something wrong but cannot quite figure out what that something could be.

There are goodbyes and thanks (for letting us see her). The attending is acting the way I've seen him act when we've consulted on patients we have no business seeing.

We cannot help her.

Surgery is not part of her plan.

And as we walk away, my burning feeling niggles so much that I cannot ignore it. A human in a bed. A herd of cattle staring at her, whispering. Trying to figure out if there is something we can cut open and sew back together.

So the crowd wanders off. But for a second I linger. We make eye contact and I smile. I want her to feel seen. Bear witness to her story. Linger in a human moment that has nothing to do with medicine.

I realize this is all to make me feel better.

She looks up and I feel it takes everything she has to meet my face and then smile back. But when she does her eyes light up. Her mouth matches the shape in the photo beside the bed and I realize immediately it's obviously her. But more than obviously the woman in the photos, her real life smile connects with another part of my brain. A both stressed and relieved part. A happy part. And then I remember.

That smile. That relieved smile. Over a year ago. The day I delivered a baby in a snowstorm.

The day that baby's cries caused my milk to come through my still breastfeeding shirt and we all laughed. My laugh, the completely nervous energy and relief that I was holding a live screaming baby. A situation that could have ended differently.

The eyes of the woman whose baby I had delivered in a snowstorm. Whose perfect baby I held on that immense day in their life.

Now dying in front of me.

I went to every hysterical place in my tired mind in that moment.

My sons in the photograph with my husband beaming at me. A woman full of life in her 30's. A new baby. A burst of life.

And off I rushed to catch up with the herd and onto the next in our long list of patients.

Never a moment to process how absolutely devastating life can be.

D.R. Wright

Sailaja and Melissa thanks for
the belief and the push

Manufactured by Amazon.ca
Bolton, ON